GOD SENT ME

A Woman Missionary in the Jungle

SHARON PORTERFIELD

DOUGLAS WELLMAN

North Carolina

God Sent Me: A Woman Missionary in the Jungle
© 2022 Sharon Porterfield and Douglas Wellman. All rights reserved.

This story is told from the author's experience and perspective.

Published in the United States by WriteLife Publishing
(an imprint of Boutique of Quality Books Publishing Company, Inc.)
www.writelife.com

978-1-60808-277-3 (p)
978-1-60808-278-0 (e)

Library of Congress Control Number: 2022940204

Book design by Robin Krauss, www.bookformatters.com
Cover Design by Rebecca Lown, www.rebeccalowndesign.com
Douglas Wellman author photo by Alisha Shaw
Editor: Michelle Booth

This book is dedicated to the Lord most of all, and to my biological family: my sister Merrilee; my children Kelly, Shelly, and Bradley; my grandchildren Trevor, Kiana, Kelsey, Malakai, Gabriel, Chloe, and Elijah Quinn; and my great grandchildren Silas, Zoey, Carson, Grayson, and Eli.

ACKNOWLEDGEMENTS

First and foremost, I want to thank the Lord who is the One who truly made this book possible by putting everything together in ways that only He can do.

I want to thank Doug Wellman, who said "Yes" to the Lord when asked if he would be interested in writing this book, and each person that he's worked with to make it possible, particularly editor, Michelle Booth, cover designer, Rebecca Lown, layout designer, Robin Krauss and publisher Terri Leidich.

I want to thank my church, Calvary Chapel St. George, who not only encouraged me, but also made this financially possible.

I want to thank Ron Case, who said from the beginning that he would help me in any way I needed because he was glad God called me and not him . . . and he has!

I want to thank my Karen family the Lord has given me, and all Karen He has brought into my life, for their amazing resilience and love that has taught me more than I could ever teach them.

I want to thank my high school friend, Barbara, who asked me after she gave her life to Jesus, "What do you think of Jesus?," then told me of Bible Study Fellowship (Women's Bible study Fellowship at that time in 1971), which prompted me to go see what it was about and brought me to give my life to Jesus, too.

I want to thank each person the Lord used in my life to bring me to Him, beginning with all who invited me to Sunday School and church through my school years. Also, those who discipled me through BSF, church and Navigators, to give me such a wonderful strong foundation in God's Word.

I want to thank everyone who said "You should write a book" so the thought was even birthed to be able to glorify my Lord this way!

I want to thank my biological family, who have been so supportive and visited me.

FOREWORD

"I want you to come back here . . ."

Picture a feisty, five-foot one-and-a-half-inch tall, forty-five-year-old single mom from Southern California, in some of the most unforgiving, unwelcoming, unhealthy and truly unsafe territory around, and that is the setting for this true story.

Sharon trudges through the war-torn jungle border between Thailand and then Burma (now Myanmar) after being told countless times, Americans are really not allowed to be here by armed guards at check points. Time after time our group of ten Americans, led by a Karen "guide" prayerfully went through check points, to see and to care for the men, women, boys and girls caught in the middle of this undeclared (and unknown) war. Some of those with rifles were held by boys barely in their teens, but knew all too well that if they did not hold their ground, they, the Karen people, would be forced out of their long-held land for good.

In a very real sense, this is a war story, and while much of it was fought with rifles and there is an element of genocide included in this story, the real war was spiritual and Sharon knew that the Lord had called her to be a part of it—and not a bit part—but hopefully, a significant role.

In Sharon's first trip to the area, and one intended to expose us Californians to some real spiritual needs and, at the very least, to come home and be more burdened to pray for and perhaps support the cause, Sharon sensed the Lord communicate to her. Not only was it a good thing for her to come on this trip, but in fact, His message to her was: "I want you to come back here . . . "

That message to Sharon was in April of 1985, and for over thirty-eight years now, she has done just that. Not only did she "go back there" later that year, but she stayed. She has learned the language, had a couple brushes with death, lived with and ministered to the Karen people in and around Thailand.

Pastor Greg Laurie, founder of Harvest Christian Fellowship with campuses in Southern California, challenged the congregation in the fall of 1984 from Isaiah 6:8: "Also I heard the voice of the Lord saying:' Whom shall I send, and who will go for us? Then I said, "Here I am! Send me." He said, 'Go and tell this people.'" Pastor Greg asked who of us would be willing to go for the Lord, no matter where it was. He asked us to stand to our feet and to state our willingness to the Lord in prayer that "He could send me."

Soon after we were given an opportunity to put some feet to our faith an "exposure" trip to Thailand was announced a few months later. All who were interested were to meet after church to discuss the trip.

As I remember, a few dozen of us attended, heard all the trips ins and outs (including its cost) and were told to go home and to pray about going on the trip.

The trip began at the far northern region of Thailand, where we were exposed to several different tribal villages as we headed south to the last villages, which were Karen villages. Later we found out that the predominantly Christian Karen people that had been living in the region were forcefully being pushed out by the now burgeoning communist Burmese government.

The conflict has been described as one of the world's "longest running civil wars" where the independent Karen, living in their homeland, referred to as Kawthoolei, were slowly but surely (and silently to the rest of the world) being pushed into Thailand.

Against all odds, and knowing all of this and more, Sharon's reply to "I want you to come back here" was a resounding YES. The pages of this book record how a woman missionary in the jungle came to know that God had sent her and how regularly He came through for her.

Pastor Ron Case
Associate Pastor, Harvest Christian Fellowship

CHAPTER ONE

FLEE!

The Lord shall preserve your going out and your coming in
from this time forth, and even forevermore.
Psalm 121:8

BURMA, 1997

The news spread quickly, "The Burmese are coming! The Burmese are coming!" Life had been fairly peaceful in Ah Moe village for the past two years, since the last time we had a warning like that. Back then, five villages fled to the safety of Thailand, but we were able to return after three months and resume teaching at our Christian mission school. The peace was about to end. This time a massive Burmese military force was on its way with one goal in mind, the extermination of the Karen people. Burma, now known by many as Myanmar, had been engaged in one of the world's longest civil wars—forty-eight years at that point—with no sign of peace on the horizon. I had made this war zone my home for over a decade for one simple reason: God sent me here.

Prior to World War II, Burma had been under the control of the United Kingdom. As was the case in countries around the world, many indigenous people resented the colonial government and began to militantly push for self-rule. On

January 4, 1948, the Union of Burma, now called Myanmar, was granted independence from the United Kingdom, but many ethnic minorities, including the Karen people the Lord had sent me to help, believed they were not represented by the parliamentary government set up to rule the new country. Insurrections continued. In 1962, after a coup d'état, the parliamentary government was replaced by a military junta. The result was a tragic abuse of power that continues to this day. The Burmese Army daily and systematically shoots on sight, kills, tortures, rapes, and unjustly imprisons the Karen people—the people I have grown to love.

Everything in this sweltering jungle in Southeast Asia was under dispute, including its name. It had once been called Karen State, Burma, but the Burmese government had renamed the northern part, Kayin State, Myanmar. The new name did nothing to solve the old problem. Control of the long, narrow stretch of jungle on the Thailand-Burma border had been hotly contested since 1949. There were several ethnic tribes throughout Burma then and each had their own land which, during World War II, the British military promised they could keep. The Karen people claimed this land as their own ethnic state that they called Kawthoolei. However, the Burmese government pushed in and wanted them out, and the government was intent on accomplishing that by any means possible. When the Burmese arrived this day, we knew they would bring violence and bloodshed.

I was not interested in politics and never had been. My heart was only to spread the Word of God and disciple. The Karen wanted to learn English so I taught it, with the Bible as my textbook. I taught in one village school for six years, then with the help of some local Karen pastors, prayer, and the Lord leading me to an amazing supporter, we built a Christian mission school in another village, called Ah Moe. Six children had come to live with me at the first village, then we all moved to Ah Moe village to live on the Christian school compound where I taught. Some children came from their homes to attend school, some came from villages very far away and stayed in dorms, and ten ended up living with me in my small bamboo home next to the river. They were my primary concern. I believed that God had chosen these children and gave them to me to care for them.

Thanks to the forewarning by the Karen soldiers that the Burmese soldiers were coming, we had a few minutes to prepare to flee. That isn't much time to consider which of your worldly possessions to take with you when you have no idea if you will ever return to your home. On the other hand, it's an eternity when compared to the possibility of the Burmese Army arriving with no warning at all.

Being a Christian missionary in a Southeast Asian war zone was never on my "to-do" list, but this was where God sent me, and because God sent me, I had no fear. I had no idea what was going to happen in the immediate future, but I was certain that God didn't send me here to allow me to be killed. I knew I must continue to obey Him and do what He had sent me to do as faithfully and calmly as possible under the circumstances. That meant I must take care of the children that God had put in my care. I would take care of my Karen children and have faith that God would take care of the Burmese Army.

It wasn't long before Karen Army troops began arriving with outboard motor-powered canoes to evacuate us. We began before dawn, but the canoes weren't very large and didn't hold many people. The plan was to put as many of the Karen as possible in each canoe without tipping it over, drop them off two hours downriver, and then return to take another load of villagers. At this point we weren't as much concerned about completely escaping the Burmese as we were about just staying ahead of them. We would leapfrog down the river by canoe until we had put a safe distance between us and our tormentors. Everyone was finally evacuated from Ah Moe and several other villages and transported downriver until we reached a village a safe distance away from the Burmese two days later. Our objective now was to cross into Thailand where we would be safe. There would be no more transportation by water; from this point we would need to walk the mountainous dirt paths, and sometimes make our own paths, through the jungle to get to the border.

We slept on the ground a safe distance away from the river that night with the intention of setting out on foot for Thailand the next morning, but even that simple plan was foiled. The principal of our mission school, Thera Doh Tha Gay, woke up with a bad case of malaria and was unable to travel. We didn't want to stay there, but we certainly couldn't leave him behind. We kept him under mosquito netting and nursed him for three days, digging holes, filling them with wood to put our cooking pots over, and cooking whatever food we could find. This was another exercise in faith. No matter what hardship has befallen me over the years I have found that if I cling to my faith in God, He will never let me down. Thera Doh Gay finally recovered his strength and we started our journey on foot.

The heat and humidity of the jungle is oppressive most of the year, and without electricity to even have a fan, we were wet from the humidity both day and night. We say we have three seasons: hot, hotter, and hottest. It was during our very short, relatively cooler, season that we were fleeing, so we were very grateful for that. Burma and Thailand are beautiful countries, wonderful examples of God's creation, with vibrant green jungle foliage, rice fields, and cool streams for bathing. However, when you are physically exhausted and have little water or nourishment, the beauty of the locale isn't necessarily the first thing you think of, so the Karen were always on the lookout for food. Having lived in the jungle all of their lives, they knew which leaves were edible, and which would make them sick—or worse.

We knew we weren't far from Thailand, but we didn't know exactly how far, when politics reared its head. The Thais, while sympathetic to the plight of the Karen, were also very protective of their border. Over and over again we would get close to a border checkpoint only to be told that we couldn't cross and had to go farther back again. We walked back and forth several times until the Thai guards finally gave us permission to cross into the safety of Thailand because they realized the Burmese Army was only one hour behind us on foot. Our escape had taken six weeks. Six weeks walking through the jungle with only the food we could find around us, such as plants, shrimps, and pollywogs. Through God's grace we all survived. Now we could finally cross into Thailand.

There was only one problem: me.

The Karen were villagers and I was not. I traveled on an American passport and had the same requirements for obtaining visas that any other foreign traveler is subject to. I wanted to accompany the Karen into Thailand with the least amount of drama possible; however, a middle-aged white woman among Karen refugees was bound to stand out and draw some attention. Attention was the last thing I wanted at that point. I needed to get to the safety of Thailand quickly and work out the rest of it later, so the Karen helped me cross the border in disguise. I donned a Karen sarong, a baggy, long-sleeved blouse, and pulled a floppy hat down over my eyes, then got in the middle of the crowd with the Karen and we all headed for the border.

Things went fine for a while until a man walked up to me and lifted my hat. "Who is this?" He asked. No one responded. He asked again, "Who is this?" We all remained silent and kept walking. He said nothing more and let us continue. (Years later I found out he knew exactly who I was, but chose only to tease me, not to intervene! The Lord protected me!)

After another hour of exhausting walking, things got worse. It began to rain. We were ordered to stop for the night because of the storm, but we had nothing to protect us from the elements.

We gathered under the jungle trees for as much cover as possible, and made beds out of leaves on the cold, wet ground. Even in those miserable conditions it was good to rest. It rained all night.

The next morning, we were awakened by the Thai guards and told we would be taken to a place where we could cook. It turned out to be an amazingly beautiful location with waterfalls and a river. We cooked some food we had scavenged and headed to the river for a much-needed bath and to wash some clothes. Doing laundry isn't too hard when you have little more than what is on your back. Eventually we were gathered together again and told to resume our walk. We had absolutely no idea where we were.

The Thai guards told us which way to go and we went without argument or question. I had no idea if we would be walking for hours or days. Despite all of the hardship, I had God's peace and knew He would take care of us all.

We walked and walked until I finally noticed a sign of civilization on the horizon: a TV antenna. If there was a TV antenna, there had to be a village nearby; I knew we must be near something.

The Thai guards finally directed us into an area they had set aside for us to construct a makeshift refugee camp. It was desolate, barren, and by now, the hottest season of the year. It had absolutely nothing, just bare, flat dirt ground with some small brush. The starkness of the location, and being counted as we walked past the Thai guards, reminded me of a concentration camp, but it was certainly better than being captured by the Burmese Army. We laid down our straw mats to sleep on in the open, but first, it was time to give thanks for our safety. Thera Doh Tha Gay was also a pastor, so he organized a service that night—a very special service.

It was Good Friday. Yes, God is good. All the time.

Thailand is half a globe away from my former home of Southern California, but there is also a distance that can't be measured in miles. It's a distance of culture and language amid poverty that is so immense it is impossible for outsiders to imagine it. As a young girl I knew such places existed, but I never gave them much thought. I certainly never considered giving up my life of wealth and fun to live in a place where I would one day consider simple things like indoor plumbing a luxury. In fact, that part of my life was actually getting worse. I had been using outhouses in the jungle up until then. Some had four walls, some had three, some had two, and some had only one. Now we just had small bushes to try to hide behind as far away from the camp as we were allowed to go. So much for pride.

Our flight from the Burmese lasted more than seven weeks until we arrived in Thailand in 1997. I always knew we would be safe. This was another of my many exercises in faith.

The Bible tells us that faith is the belief in things unseen. That's quite true, of course, but that doesn't mean we can't experience God's presence. If we listen, He will speak to us. Not in words necessarily, but by His pulling at our heart that guides us in His direction. Sometimes we are pulled in a direction we are reluctant to go. We may be insecure. We may be unsure. Ultimately, it comes down to a matter of faith. When we know that God is directing our steps we walk in faith. It was by faith and confirmations (I had four), that I knew God was calling me to a ministry in Burma and Thailand. Faith took me there, and it's my continuing faith that has kept me there. This hasn't been an easy task. In fact, sometimes it was quite difficult and even dangerous. However, I knew God sent me there so I knew He would protect me.

What follows next is not just a story about me, but a story about what God has done through me, and sometimes, in spite of me. There have been trials and tribulations, great sadness and great joy, and in all of this I never doubted for a moment that God's will was being fulfilled in my life. I wouldn't have had it any other way.

CHAPTER TWO

SEARCHING FOR GOD

Your eyes saw my substance, being yet unformed.
And in Your book they all were written,
The days fashioned for me, when as yet there were none of them.

Psalm 139:16

SOUTHERN CALIFORNIA - 1941

E nding up as a missionary is about as far away from my beginnings as I could get. As a child I wasn't raised with the knowledge of Jesus as my Savior. In fact, it was the opposite. I guess I'm an example of God meeting us where we are and taking us where He wants us to be. For that mercy I am grateful.

I entered this world on June 19, 1941 at Hollywood Hospital in the city of Los Angeles. The Great Depression wasn't all that far in the past, and many families were still recovering. My father served in the Merchant Marines in World War II. After the war, and the preceding economic depression, many people were still struggling, but I was fortunate to have been the daughter of an incredibly hardworking man who was a blessing to our family. His name was Allen O'Brien and he had an inauspicious start in the post-war world of business. He didn't have much more than a great work ethic and a good pair of shoes when he began walking residential neighborhoods selling pots and pans door-to-door, but he was successful and smart. He parlayed his earnings into a partnership in an electronics wholesale business that did very well. In fact, it did so well that he was able to retire at the age of forty-five. He was a moral and generous man and he took good care of his family. As a child in the 1950s I had an allowance of one hundred dollars a month, a great sum in those days when a soda fountain drink was five cents and a movie ticket was a quarter. Like many young people who are long on money and short on responsibility, I picked up a rebellious streak and built my non-school hours around things that were fun, but not necessarily good. Fortunately, the temptations of that fairly peaceful era were not the deadly ones that children face today.

My mother's name was Helen Wilson and she had a pretty good childhood. Her father was the principal of Monrovia High School and her mother was a housewife, content to raise my mom and her brother Ronald. It was a church-going home and Mother was forced to attend church on Sunday, but she rebelled when she got older and stopped going.

My parent's spiritual journey, if you can call it that, progressed from being atheists to evolutionists. While that wasn't necessarily good for me, it wasn't entirely bad, either.

My father was strongly motivated to search for truth. I always thought of my father as something of an adventurer, a searcher, perhaps. I think I picked up that trait from him, but as a young person my searching was pretty limited; I was only searching for fun. If it wasn't fun, I wasn't interested. It would be many years before I would consider the broader, more complex issues of life. As a child I believed that there must be a Creator because I could see the world was far too big and complex to be an accident. My parents didn't attend church but, to their credit, they didn't stop me from doing so. From the age of five I began walking to Sunday school on my own, and I continued to explore religion throughout my adolescence, right into college, where I took a class on religion. I didn't follow a specific religious philosophy and I didn't believe Jesus was the Son of God, but I believed in something. Exactly what "something" was remained to be seen.

Since my father was retired and financially secure by the time I was in high school, we were able to indulge in his passion for exploring other cultures. We traveled a lot as a family, and Father did a great deal of exploring on his own. He joined the famous paleoanthropologist and archaeologist Louis B. Leaky on several of his digs in Africa where he was looking for an evolutionary trail from ancient animal fossils to modern man. He is even mentioned in the Leaky biography, *Leaky's Luck*. Despite his association with the famous scientist and his personal experience with the specimens and data they collected, I don't think my father was ever entirely satisfied that he had found complete truth in all matters. He retained a searching mind for his entire life.

Unfortunately, some of these cultural advantages were lost on me. I wasn't all that excited about traveling to begin with, and I never really liked the tropical weather on the islands we frequently visited. My goal was to have fun with my friends. As my father became more successful, we moved twice to nicer neighborhoods. My parents were a bit status conscious and encouraged me to be friends with the wealthier children, but I didn't want to choose my friends based on their parents' financial assets. As a result, I had a lot more friends on the lower rungs of the economic ladder than I had at the top. That might have been part of my rebellious streak. That was pretty much the story of my young life: rebellion and fun.

My parents lived in unbelief, but they didn't force it on me. They never spoke of religion, but even in the spiritual darkness of my family home, I knew there had to be a God. It seemed obvious to me. We live in a beautiful, amazing world and that was evident to me even at the tender age of five. I just couldn't possibly believe that the variety of creatures and plants, all living together and depending upon one another for survival, could be happenstance. How could the caterpillar that turns into a butterfly and the thundering rhinoceros both come from the same random accident that produced life? There had to be a Creator. There had to be a God. My parents didn't assist in my research, but they also didn't hinder it, and my father's demand for indisputable evidence on all matters likely rubbed off on me. The fact that there was a Creator God was perfectly evident to me, but Jesus was another matter. I could not accept him as the Son of God because the "scientific evidence" didn't support it. How could there be a virgin birth? How could he die and rise from the grave? My mind was rooted in things that I could see and touch. It would be years before I fully understood that our world is not entirely physical. Nevertheless, Sunday mornings would find me in a church somewhere. Most of my friends came from church-going homes and attended a variety of different churches. In my heart I knew that attending church was the right thing for me to do, so I tagged along with them. I attended Baptist, Presbyterian, Methodist, Lutheran, Catholic, and Episcopalian churches and I felt one was good as the other. As long as I was in church, I felt I was on the right track. I knew what I was hearing was good, but I just couldn't accept it all. I was still looking for proof.

My teenage years were fairly typical, although privileged. It would be nice if I could say I was a good student, but that wouldn't be true. Scholarship took second place to my social life by a healthy margin. As a result, not only was I not much of a student, but my grades were starting to make it look like I wouldn't get into a college. Naturally, this didn't make my parents very happy. They wanted the best for me and in their minds that meant a college education. To sharpen my academic focus, I was enrolled in Girls Collegiate High School in Claremont, California, where my grades improved to the point that I became "college acceptable material." Upon graduation I was accepted at Stephens College in Columbia, Missouri, at the time, a college for women only. I liked Stephens very much. Rather than being held to a strict academic program, Stephens allowed me a great deal of freedom to select the subjects I wanted to study. A regimented academic program probably would have annoyed the rebellious part of me, but being free to choose classes that really interested me was perfect.

One of my first choices was a class in religion, but there I was confronted by the same old problem: how could I believe in the miracles described in the Bible when they didn't conform to the reality of the physical world? I took my questions to my professor. "How can I believe in the virgin birth?" I asked. He replied, "Either you do or you don't. You have to make a choice." That was absolutely no help. I responded as a young adult firmly grounded in "reality." "Well then," I said, "if you can't prove it, I don't believe it." I was right back to where I started.

Despite my problems accepting the divinity of Jesus and the associated miracles, I hadn't given up on God. I began attending a Unitarian church in Columbia, near the Stephens campus. The Unitarian philosophy allowed me to believe in the things I could accept without being compelled to accept the things I couldn't believe. I remained in the Unitarian church for the rest of my college days, and when I graduated and moved back to California, I wanted to attend a Unitarian church in Riverside. My father accompanied me to that church and at the conclusion of the service he analyzed the experience for me. The problem, as he saw it, was that the Unitarians had man-made rules—rules that weren't in the Bible—like every other church he had attended. He wasn't looking for a word from man; he was looking for a word from God. I had to admit that he had a point. I stopped going to the Unitarian church.

My father never completely turned his back on the concept of God. He was remarkably open-minded in that regard. He continued to search and be open to the possibility that there might be an all-powerful divine creator who loves us and cares about us. After I became a Christian, he asked me many questions about the Bible. Unfortunately, as a relatively new Christian, I didn't have the in-depth answers that he sought. I answered his questions as best I could and he continued to seek. He began watching the telecasts of Calvary Chapel in Costa Mesa, California, which was then pastored by Chuck Smith. He also accompanied me to a Christian seminar, but in his opinion the speaker was just a good, clever salesman. He was adept at coming up with the answers to questions and the solutions to problems that he created in his examples, which were the truth, but my dad didn't believe. Whether he actually accepted the Lord or not I don't know, since he was killed in a plane crash shortly thereafter. I have always hoped and prayed that he turned his life over to Jesus before, or even while, he went down in that airplane.

A college education was all well and fine, but I believed that true happiness would come with marriage. A marriage with children would be ultimate happiness. The transition from college student to housewife didn't take too long. I had known my future husband, Don, since middle school. We married and settled in San Bernardino, California. Children followed. Kelly, in 1962, Shelly, in 1964, and Bradley in 1966. I became a typical, average American suburban housewife and I was perfectly happy. We had friends, we had family, and everything was just fine.

After eight years and three wonderful children, thoughts of a loving God came back into the forefront of my life. They were sparked by a question from my childhood friend, Barbara. I had attended a Roman Catholic Church with her when we were in high school, but in the ensuing years she had begun attending Women's Bible Study Fellowship, became a Christian, and was baptized. We were talking when she visited one day and she asked me a question: what did I think about Jesus? "Well, I think He is a great guy . . . good teacher . . . what He taught was right and good, but definitely not the Son of God."

"Okay," she said, "I guess this Bible study isn't for you." And that was the end of that. For a while.

I thought about our conversation after she left and I was bothered by it. *I don't think it's up to her to decide what's good for me or not*, I thought to myself. Whether this was the Holy Spirit working on me, or my rebellious nature, I don't know, but I decided to find out where the Women's Bible Study Fellowship was being held and go check it out for myself. Barbara lived in San Clemente, but her sister-in-law, Julie, was one of my best friends in Riverside. I called her and we went to the Bible study together. I loved it. I realized I was finally studying the truth I had been looking for.

As most Christians know, if you want to stir up the enemy against you, a surefire way is to go looking for God. Satan didn't waste any time seeing whether or not my newfound Christian interest was going to stick. The attacks started immediately. In no time, my three children were all ill with measles, mumps, and chickenpox. Fortunately, the leader of my small group was sensitive to my situation and faithful to support me during this difficult time of trial. She didn't allow my family obligations and problems to hinder my progress. In addition to the group discussions which I was missing, we also had homework assignments. She would send the homework to me and call every week to see how I was doing on it. She always made sure that I got the upcoming lessons. We were studying the Minor Prophets in the Old Testament then, and we spent a great deal of time talking about the lessons. Being somewhat new, I had many, many questions and she was faithful to take the time to answer them to the best of her abilities, until the Bible study stopped in June for a summer break.

That summer my husband remained rooted in unbelief and was showing signs of unhappiness. The stress from his unhappiness ultimately resulted in a separation. This was difficult for me, of course, but I hoped the marriage would be saved. I took the children to visit my parents in Newport Beach, California for a month and we all had a wonderful time. When we returned, I was very happy and confident that everything was going to work out fine. There was one new issue, however. We had become very unhappy with the quality of education our children were receiving in the public schools and wanted to make a change. One of our neighbors had enrolled their children in Riverside Christian Day School and was very pleased with it, so we enrolled our children there as well. I was happy with this arrangement and within two months all three children and I had prayed and accepted Jesus Christ as our Lord and Savior through studying God's Word.

When the Women's Bible Study Fellowship returned in September, I found the "proof" I was looking for. We were studying the Book of Matthew and I realized that all of the prophecies that we read in the Minor Prophets had been precisely fulfilled. It was absolutely *impossible* for this to have happened randomly. Only the divine hand of a Creator operating from outside our physical universe could have structured these events so precisely and announced them hundreds of years in advance. My question about the virgin birth had finally been answered. It was, indeed, a miracle. Jesus was born in the exact place and at the exact time as it was prophesied so many years before. All of a sudden, I realized that Jesus really is the Son of God. What a profound moment! Everything has been wonderful in my heart from that time on. The emptiness in my life was behind me. I finally found fulfillment and joy that has remained with me to this day. I became a new person in Jesus!

During the next couple of years, the children and I continued in our Christian growth. I wasn't entirely happy with the quality of the preaching in our church—it seemed to lack biblical focus—but we had been attending for a number of years. A few years before I became a Christian, the pastor of the church asked me if I would be interested in becoming a youth advisor. That didn't seem like a very good idea. I told him that I didn't know the Bible well enough, but he assured me that I would do just fine. It wasn't so much about my knowledge of the Bible, he told me, but about my ability to listen to young people. That made sense to me, and my own children would be teenagers soon, so getting a little practical experience in advance would no doubt be helpful. I just hoped that they wouldn't be the way I was at their age. I took the ministry and got enormous satisfaction from working with the youth. I became their counselor and confident, but more importantly, I developed enduring friendships, some of them I still have to this day.

One of the guaranteed consequences of a true walk with

the Lord is a change in lifestyle. We want to become Christ-like, which sounds like an impossibility, and to some degree is, yet we consciously change things in our lives to conform to the teachings of Jesus because we love Him. We don't become sinless, far from it, but sin makes us uncomfortable. It's impossible to maintain our old sinful habits without nagging pangs of conscience. We don't want that sinful life anymore, so we change our lifestyle. So it was with me. I began to eliminate those things from my life that I felt were spiritually questionable. We had always had an active social life, but I quit drinking and we stopped having an annual drinking party in our home. I slowly eliminated everything from my life that I thought was counter to my increasingly strengthening Christian beliefs. This included many things that my husband enjoyed. I guess I should have anticipated that this would eventually become a big problem, but to the contrary, I was quite happy and felt everything was just fine. In fact, when the final rift in our marriage came, it caught me completely by surprise.

In the summer of 1973, our children were going off to camp and I was looking forward to two weeks alone with my husband. That wasn't to be. The day after the children left for camp my husband walked out on me. I was shocked and devastated. Emotionally shattered, I was sure my life was over. As I looked for something to hang onto, I came across two books which I believe the Lord sent into my life to strengthen me. Ironically, considering its importance at the time, I can't remember the name of the first book, but it was about two halves of an eggshell fitting together, with weaknesses and strengths complementing each other, making a relationship complete. It helped me to understand how two people could think differently, yet fit together. The other book was entitled, *From Prison to Praise*, by Merlon Carruthers. It really helped me to change my attitude—

to keep my eyes on Jesus—and taught me that even if I didn't feel like thanking God for my current situation, I could, and should, do it. Thankfulness would eventually come naturally as I learned to accept His will. It was hard, yet the process of spiritual growth was working.

When we face a devastating personal rejection it's common for people to feel they have no value in any area. I was no exception. The failure of my marriage made me feel like a failure as a human being. Worse, I felt as though the Lord could no longer use my life for Him. Looking back, it was foolish for me to believe that any human conflict could separate me from the love of the Lord, but we don't always think clearly when we are in the depths of emotional devastation. Nevertheless, at that low point in my life I felt I had no value and I began to consider whether or not I wanted to continue to live. Fortunately, one of my friends "just happened" to call.

Realizing the seriousness of my situation, she called another friend and they came to surround me with support and prayer. I believe the Lord sent them, of course. Loneliness and isolation are tools Satan uses to crush us. Our defense is the support of caring Christian friends and I thank God that they were sent into my life at that moment. It was at this point that I first began to understand the meaning of Romans 8:28: "And we know that all things work together for good to those who love God, to those who are called according to his purpose." Perhaps, above all else, this verse brings reassurance and comfort to believers who understand that we are never defeated when we maintain our faith in the Lord. There is always hope. That is His promise.

I know that the Lord hates divorce. The scripture says so. I prayed for two years after my husband left that he would come back. I remember the Lord telling me, "Don't pray for reconciliation. Pray for his salvation." After two years he married another woman, who was a Catholic, who also said she's a Christian. She prayed and believed it was God's will to marry him. I don't know how a Christian can believe it's God's will for a Christian to marry a non-Christian. The Bible says not to. I asked her, but afterward, the Lord told me to let it go. Once he was married again, I knew I couldn't pray for him to come back anymore. I am still praying for his salvation. After he left, the girls and I were . . . I don't know how to say this without it sounding wrong . . . but we realized we were released from an oppression. Living with an unbeliever is hard, and yet, if that is God's will, that is what we would have done. I don't believe that it was God's will for the divorce, but the girls and I have said we were able to grow in the Lord and get to know Him personally afterward. The Lord was then the center of our lives and our home. It was such a blessing to be able to pray together, serve Him together, and make decisions based on His Word for what He wanted us to do, who He wanted us to be, and how He wanted us to grow. I know that it is not His perfect will. I would have rather been married and served Him together, but God didn't answer that prayer. He has enabled us to go forward, to continue to grow in Him, to serve Him, and to glorify Him in our lives. That is another wonderful example of the grace of God and His love for us. The fact that what happened against His will does not end our lives, but He can pick up the pieces and help us go on to glorify Him.

With the emotional support of my friends and the spiritual support of His Word, I began to stabilize a bit emotionally. However, in the physical realm, my problems were anything but small, beginning with the very basics of survival. We were going to need to leave our home. I was also going to need to get a job, which would have been easier had I not still had the sudden added responsibilities of being a single parent. In the midst of this chaos, I fortunately had the blessing of good counsel from another friend, Chuck. In addition to comfort and emotional support, he was a fairly new Christian who really understood the need for good, solid biblical teaching. Chuck had joined a group that was starting a church that would explore God's Word thoroughly, and I was invited to join them, which I enthusiastically did. It's hard to describe how much that church meant to me at that particular time. Aside from the stress of having to work in a secular environment, I really needed friends who showed the love of the Lord. They came alongside me, encouraged me, and even helped me with my children. They got us through everything with their love, compassion, prayers, and teaching us God's Word.

Divorce is always hard on children and that was certainly the case with our family. We all struggled with it, but the girls and I found comfort by drawing closer to the Lord. It was not so easy for my son, Brad, however. He missed his father terribly and cried himself to sleep at night. There is nothing worse for a mother than to witness a child's agony. It became apparent that Brad really needed his father, so with a degree of trepidation I agreed he could live with Don. I guess there is never a "good" solution in custody matters; there is only the one that seems better. That was the way I felt about this situation. Although I have questioned the decision many times over the years, Brad and I, by God's grace and mercy, now have a loving parent-child relationship. Fortunately, Don didn't make any changes in the children's education. Brad was allowed to stay in Riverside Christian Day School through the eighth grade and then went to a public high school. Don also continued to pay for the girls' schooling, and they graduated from Woodcrest Christian School.

Our spiritual journey wasn't exclusively intellectual. The

church we were attending in 1975 didn't have a very big youth program. In fact, it consisted of my girls and only one other girl. This was a problem for us, but the Holy Spirit was really moving through Southern California at the time and the solution was only a one-hour car ride away. We heard that Christian bands were starting up and having concerts down at Calvary Chapel in Costa Mesa. That was exactly what the girls and I wanted and needed, so we drove down there on Saturday nights and took part in the worship. A young pastor by the name of Greg Laurie, who was from Calvary Chapel Costa Mesa, and was clearly a gifted speaker, started a small Bible study in Riverside, California, which we began to attend. That little Bible study grew to be the internationally known Harvest Christian Fellowship. We became involved with Harvest as a family and the girls went to Forest Home Christian Camp. There were a lot of struggles during this period, particularly financial, but the girls really turned to the Lord and so did I. When they graduated from high school, a government grant allowed both of them to go to Azusa Pacific, a Christian university. The Lord was faithful to provide for all our needs.

Our involvement with Harvest was a giant stepping-stone in our Christian walk. Shelly and I joined an East Coast Outreach Team through Harvest and I enjoyed going out and sharing the Gospel with people. There were so many things going on at Harvest and so many opportunities to serve. I was also involved with their street witnessing teams, and their lodging ministry, in which we took women off the street, through Harvest, to care for them and disciple them. I enjoyed serving the Lord in that ministry as I, myself, depended on Him for everything. This was a huge leap of faith, since we were in dire straits financially, because my job didn't pay much. At the end of the month when I wrote all my checks, the expenses were always more than my income. To this day I still don't know how the Lord worked all of that out, yet it has been a consistent pattern through my entire Christian life. He has always provided for all our needs. Everything. He has become my best friend. He is incredibly faithful.

I loved going to church, in fact, I guess I could say my life revolved around it. I would go as many times as I could, especially during the period when all of my children were away at college, but a specific Wednesday night service in November 1984 changed my life forever. As always, I went to learn more of God's Word, but they weren't teaching from the scriptures that night. Instead, one of the women from the church staff was showing slides. This had never happened before, so I was not paying much attention. I was just kind of looking around the sanctuary and thinking of other things. Every once in a while, I would look up at the screen and sort of listen to what she was saying, but then my mind would drift off to other thoughts. At some point I looked up at the screen and saw a picture of a bamboo hut, a very small one. It sat right in the middle of a jungle and the Lord clearly spoke to me, saying "I want you to go there." I was jolted to awareness and thought to myself, *Where is* there? I said, "Lord, you know I'm not paying attention. I don't know where *there* is." I had to find out, so when the presentation was over, I went up to the lady who had shown the slides and asked. She said, "Thailand." *Great,* I thought. *I'm a college graduate, but I don't know where Thailand is.* I decided to humble myself and ask and she said, "Do you know where Vietnam is?" "Yes," I said. "Thailand is to the west of that." "Oh, okay. Thanks." "Why are you asking me?" "No reason," I said as I headed for the door, but I didn't get very far. I heard the Lord very clearly tell me to go back and ask her when she was going back to Thailand, so I obediantly went back. Some people mock Christians for saying that the Lord speaks to them, but when He does, we know it could come from nowhere else. I dutifully went back and asked the woman when she was returning to Thailand. "Why are you asking?" she said. "No reason," I said. She told me she wasn't planning on going back. *Good*, I thought to myself. *I'm off the hook on that one.* I enjoyed working in the lodging ministry and I was happy with my life in general. Little did I know, I was about to get another lesson in the Lord's will.

My life was good, but I was a bit frustrated with my job. I wanted to stay in a Christian environment as much as possible; however, my employment situation did not conform to that desire. I had been working for a roofing company for about ten years and my coworkers didn't really appreciate my love for Jesus. That was frustrating, since for eight hours a day, five days a week, I was unable to share the faith from which I drew so much strength. My nights and weekends were filled with Christian friends, including a Bible study for singles that took place in my home every Friday night through Harvest. In general, my Christian life in Southern California was comfortable and I felt no need to go somewhere else, although I wasn't entirely opposed to the idea, either. Six months prior to this, my pastor, Greg Laurie, had given us a challenge from Isaiah 6:8: "Also I heard the voice of the Lord saying: 'Whom shall I send, and who will go for us?' Then I said, "Here I am! Send me." He said, 'Go and tell this people.'"

Greg asked who of us would be willing to go for the Lord, no matter where it was. He asked us to make a commitment in our heart if we were willing to do that, which I did. Although willing, I wasn't really expecting to go anywhere, and if I did, I was thinking it would be no farther than the East Coast, where I had been on the Harvest East Coast Outreach Team.

As the child of a well-off family, I had the opportunity to do a lot of traveling. Most people find this to be fun and exciting, but as I said before, I really didn't enjoy it. I had been to Jamaica, Hawaii, and Tahiti—we always went to tropical places. I really hated the heat and humidity and would have preferred to have stayed home with my friends. Looking back now, I can see those childhood trips were God's preparation for sending me to Thailand. He knows the end from the beginning, so it certainly wasn't an accident. I didn't think much more about the Thailand trip after that Wednesday night in November 1984. I had heard God's directive and I had followed up on it. I had done my part and it was now God's move. I knew He had told me to go there, but I thought it would be at least five years down the road. After my children had graduated from college and were married, I would have more freedom. Surely God knew this. Yes, He knew it, but we were operating off of His plan and timetable, not mine.

Two months later, in January 1985, I received a call from the woman who had shown the slides. "You were asking questions about when I would be going back to Thailand. I didn't think I was, but I believe the Lord wants me to take some people back there on an exposure trip. Do you want to go?" I was caught off guard and said the first thing that came to mind, "No." "Oh. You were asking questions, so I thought you might want to go." At this point the Lord's will overpowered mine. I explained that I didn't really want to go, but I believed that the Lord had told me to go. The woman asked me, "What are you trying to tell me?" That was a question that called for a direct answer. I told her to put my name down on her list and He would take it from there. As was beginning to be a pattern in my life, I stepped out in faith.

The exposure trip to Thailand began with training to familiarize ourselves with the land, culture, and customs of the country. The primary focus of the training was on the Lord, of course, and the classes were called Servanthood Training. The classes were excellent and I was really enjoying them. I looked forward to attending every week; then one night I was hit with another dose of reality. "Do you know the money is due in three days?" I was asked. "Ah, no. I haven't been keeping track," I responded. We were all responsible for the funds needed for the trip. I had been setting money aside as best I could, but our financial situation was always tight. I had managed to set aside $100 of the $1,275 that was about to be due. *This is going to be exciting*, I thought to myself. *What is God going to do in three days?*

Every day during my lunch break I would drive home and check my mailbox with the thought that money would miraculously be in it. I had never received money before, and I have never received it since, but in those three days I did receive two checks and some cash. I don't remember who the money was from or why they sent it. It was totally random, but now I know it was from the Lord. It only amounted to thirty-six dollars, but it was a help. However, the fact remained that I was a long way from having the money I needed for the trip. I called the woman and told her exactly how much money I had. She asked if I was positive I couldn't come up with more money. I assured her that that was the best I could do. What did she want me to do? She didn't have a solution to the problem any more than I did, so she told me to come to class that night, as usual, and we would talk more. I agreed, and felt at peace.

When I arrived back at work, I was told there was a telephone call for me. It was the woman from church. "Your trip is paid for," she said with excitement. I was stunned. "How did this happen?" I asked. She told me that she had received a telephone call from someone in the mountains, who I didn't know and who didn't know me, and he told her that the Lord had told him to pay for this exposure trip for someone who didn't have the money to go. "Do you know who that is?" he asked. "Yes, as a matter of fact I do," she told him. When we ended our call all I could think was, "Wow."

As you can imagine, I was totally energized when I got to class that night. If there was any doubt about whether God had directed me to go to Thailand, this removed it. Watching God turn this financial situation around was a classic confirmation that God's will will always be done. Since the $1,275 travel fee had been paid by God's anonymous servant, I was left with my original $136 . . . the exact amount I needed for my passport and immunization shots. To the penny.

By God's miraculous work I was on my way to Thailand.

CHAPTER THREE

A NEW LIFE

For God so loved the world that He gave His only begotten Son,
that whoever believes in Him should not perish but have everlasting life.
John 3:16

I was used to traveling, so in April of 1985, I and the exposure team climbed aboard a jet at the Los Angeles International Airport with a familiar sense of anticipation. Yet there was also something very different about this trip. Thanks to my parents' wealth and interest in travel, I had already had an opportunity to see many interesting parts of the world. Like my father, I had enjoyed learning about the different tribal cultures and watching the different ways people went about their daily lives around the world. I previously had the intellectual curiosity of a tourist, interested in the sights, sounds, colors, and smells of different countries, but not necessarily relating to the people at a personal human level. I knew this trip was unique. I would not be looking at the world from a schoolgirl's perspective this time. I would be looking at the world from God's perspective. My earthly father had paid to send me on vacation. My Heavenly Father—although I wasn't fully aware of it yet—had paid to send me off to serve Him.

The flight from Los Angeles to Bangkok took over thirty hours, with one layover, so the ten of us on the team had time to discuss our itinerary and the fact that our diet was going to change drastically. We would be eating monkey. I guess I don't have to explain how I felt about that at the time. But we talked and read and slept and I felt good because I was positive that God was sending me on this trip. He had unexpectedly spoken to my heart and paid my expenses, so His hand was clear in this. However, I had absolutely no idea what His long-term plan might be. As far as I was concerned, this was an exposure trip; I was going to be exposed to a new country and culture, and then go home. My thoughts were only on this two-week trip and learning about Thailand. Nothing beyond that. I knew I was being directed by Him so I had no concerns.

We landed in Bangkok in the middle of the night and went through the routine of retrieving luggage, showing passports, and finding our driver. Our leader already knew him from her previous trip, so it was easy to locate him. We climbed into his white van and he took us to a hotel in a tourist area. People who travel know that traffic rules can be quite different around the world, in fact, sometimes it seems like there are no rules at all. Let's just say that the trip to the hotel was "thrilling" and our driver was remarkable for his crazy passing abilities.

The humid heat hit us as soon as we got off the plane. Since our van and hotel were air conditioned, we didn't pay much attention to it at first, but it caught up with us. The next day I was quite sick, and one of the guys on the team, Ron Case, decided to help me try to find something to make me feel better. I was nauseated, one of the side effects of the malaria prevention medicine we were all taking. We walked along the hot and humid streets of Bangkok trying to find Coca-Cola and ice cream, the only things that sounded good to me. We passed many street vendors of unfamiliar foods along the way. The worst smells were the grilled cuttlefish and squid. We finally found a street vendor who had Coke. Apparently, he wanted to make sure he got the refund on the glass bottle, so he poured it into a small plastic bag, put a straw in it, and closed it with a rubber band. On I went, drinking my Coke from a plastic bag. We walked a long way before we found anything that even resembled a grocery store. We eventually located one below the sidewalk level. Venturing in, I finally found ice cream, in unfamiliar flavors such as corn and brown beans. Poking through the odd assortment, I spotted one I thought sounded decent—coconut ice cream—and devoured it. Soon after finishing it and my Coke, my nausea was gone—God's grace.

Later that day, we all began traveling in the van to the northernmost villages. We traveled all day and stopped along the way at open roadside "restaurants" for our meals and saw many unfamiliar sights, like flies on the meat being butchered, and rats in the kitchens.

We spent our first night on the road in a huge wooden house. The guys slept on one side of the big, open wooden floor upstairs, and the girls slept on the other side. We were all lined up facing each other. The bathroom consisted of a "squat potty" and a huge concrete water tank with a bucket in it. Many went in before I did and said nothing when they came out. When I went in, I had no idea how to use either one. I decided to come back out and humble myself by asking how to use them, instead of embarrassing myself even more by using them incorrectly. I found out that I was supposed bathe by standing next to the water tank, not getting into it, and using the small bucket to scoop the water out of the tank and pour it over me. I did as instructed and got the entire bathroom floor wet, which was how the system worked. I also had to learn how to position myself over the squat potty. I am so glad I asked—everywhere else we went had the same system and it was located outside of the building!

We traveled over primitive dirt roads to many different tribal villages—Lisu, Lahu, Hmong, and Aka—and woke up in all of them in the dark to the squealing sound of pigs being killed to feed us. At one village, women were bathing and washing their clothes in the river wearing only sarongs and no tops; some villages had neat fences, but most didn't. One had no water supply that I saw, and all were covered in red dust. They were hot and sticky, but the beauty of the people won my heart. It was so different traveling as a Christian and caring about the people and their culture. I couldn't get enough.

On the seventh day of the trip, the ten of us packed ourselves into our white van and drove from northern Thailand down to the central part of the country. The trip took all day over roads that were paved, unpaved, and sometimes worse. The weather was hot and humid, but the beauty of the country leapt out at me as we made our slow journey south. Until a couple of months previously, I didn't even know where Thailand was located, and now I was driving through it learning firsthand about the geography, beautiful flowers, and trees. Thanks to its monsoon climate, the country is incredibly green, lush, and beautiful. There are more than 25,000 varieties of trees, plants, and flowers that filled the air with the unique aroma I had never experienced before. We met the people close-up, remarking about their colorful clothing and their daily activities. The Thai people went about their lives as we drove through their towns and villages, so we saw them as they really were. There were many spirit houses along the way where the Buddhists feed the spirits to keep them happy so they would protect them. The trip was simultaneously exhausting and exhilarating. We spent one night in Bangkok, then headed out the next day to our last destination. It began to rain and the farther we drove the worse the storm got. By the time we pulled into Htee Kee Village at 9:00 p.m., the storm had become a full-fledged monsoon that obscured any light from the moon and stars. It was pitch black and the brutal rain was relentless. We had reached our destination.

We scrambled out of our van and ran through the mud and rain into a wooden house on stilts. We were welcomed by a small group of village people all speaking a language I had never heard before and certainly couldn't understand. We all found places to sit and I listened to our hosts converse while I silently asked myself, *What am I, or we, supposed to be doing?* The Lord spoke to me very clearly and said, "I want you to come back here."

That wasn't the answer I was expecting. I thought, *Lord, you did it to me again! I don't even know where I am!* Perplexed, I turned to our church team leader and whispered, "Where are we?" "Why?" she asked. "Well, it seems like the Lord just told me He wants me to come back here. What do I do?" I guess she was just as surprised as I was. She said, "Do nothing. Stay quiet. Don't say one word to anybody. Just pray about it." I was happy with that answer. I trusted God.

By this point in my life, I was fully aware that when God calls on us to do something, He provides the means for us to do it. The fact that He had provided the money for the exposure trip was the most recent example in my life. On the other hand, I was sitting in a wooden house on stilts in a torrential downpour, in a place I probably couldn't even find on a map, surrounded by people speaking a language I couldn't understand. Under the circumstances it didn't seem unreasonable to ask Him a couple of questions. I started with my biggest concern. "Lord, what about my kids?" He answered, "They are old enough. I can take better care of them than you can now." My youngest was nineteen, so I knew that was very true. My second question was, "What about the house?" God had given me a wonderful house that we used for our church lodging ministry where the Lord provided a home for needy and abused women and hosted a weekly Bible study. God had provided that house for us and He said He would take care of it, too. "Okay," I said, "that's really all I have." I had my answers. I didn't pray about it anymore.

The next day we began ministering to the people in the next village, Htee Hta. It was extremely hot and humid all day and night. It never cooled down, but we walked through the village meeting people for the next four days. Our host family could speak English and translated for us. Like many ministry teams, we had some medical personnel with us to provide some basic health care to the villagers we met. Our two nurses and one doctor would do their best to diagnose and treat medical problems with the limited resources they had available to them. What would seem to us to be the most rudimentary, basic health care was really an enormous blessing to these people who had minimum to no healthcare at all. One of the patients—a man from the Arakanese tribal group of Burma—was brought to the doctor in serious condition. He had been conscripted into the Burmese Army about ten years before and was essentially being held against his will. After a decade of war, he couldn't take it anymore and decided to run to the other side to escape the constant fighting. He made it, but not without injury. The Burmese opened fire on him as he fled, but succeeded only in shooting off part of one of his fingers. Unfortunately, by the time he got to our doctor his finger was gangrenous. The only treatment option was surgery, and there was no anesthetic available in the village. What served as an operating room was very small and hot. I'm no good watching people in pain, so I stayed outside and prayed for him during the operation. They explained to him that we came to Thailand because we love Jesus and we want everyone to know that Jesus loves them, too. Whatever help we can bring to the people is done in Jesus' name as a symbol of His love. The man understood and went into surgery. The patient wasn't the only one who suffered during that operation. The doctor had never performed surgery on a patient that had not been anesthetized and he realized that the surgery was going to be excruciatingly painful, a fact that wore heavily on him. He was used to treating pain, not causing it, and the surgery was as agonizing for him emotionally as it was for the patient physically. He left the operating room several times, running past where I was praying, to relieve his nausea. Nevertheless, patient and doctor both survived the unpleasant experience. The doctor decided his time in Thailand was up and he left the next day. The patient remained in the hospital to recuperate and we continued ministering around that village. Fortunately, the story doesn't end there. The following month another team from Harvest went to Htee Hta village and looked in on the man. His finger was completely healed. The love shown to this man had a profound impact on him as well as the villagers. He gave his heart to Jesus and was baptized in the local river by the pastor on the team. I don't know if that doctor ever realized that his work had helped save that man's soul, not just his body.

It's not just the villagers who occasionally need medical treatment. Missionaries have the same human frailties as everyone else, and in my decades of ministry I have had my share of medical problems. The first one occurred on this trip when I was bitten by a scorpion. If you've never been bitten by a scorpion, I suggest you do your best to keep it that way. If you have been bitten, you know how horribly painful it is. This was my first scorpion bite and I didn't know what to do other than stay with our host in their wooden house. Three of my colleagues stopped by at different times and asked if anyone had prayed for me. When I responded that I hadn't been prayed for, they left. Finally, as the third person was walking away, I said, "Why did you ask me? I told you no one prayed for me and you kept walking on?" "Oh yeah," he responded, and called the whole team back. They gathered around me to pray for me and I soon felt a little better. His response made me laugh later.

Our host then came toward me and immediately got my undivided attention. She was carrying a knife and sharpening it on what appeared to be a piece of charcoal. Instantly I had visions of being cut open and having the poison sucked out of me like one would do for a snakebite. I didn't like that idea at all, and it apparently showed in my face. She noticed my alarm and calmed me down with the explanation that she wasn't going to use the knife on me, she was only going to use the piece of "charcoal." To this day I don't know why she had that knife in her hand, but it certainly made me jump to a scary conclusion. Far from being sliced open, the treatment was actually quite simple. The material that looked like charcoal was a special herb, she told me, as she wet it and placed it on my bite so it would draw the poison out of my body. Then a well-meaning but unknowing person on my team came by and took it off asking, "What is this?" So much for getting the poison drawn out anymore.

When God decides He wants to teach you something you don't necessarily get sick days off. I was still in a bit of pain from the scorpion bite, but the team was going to travel by boat to visit an animist village that night and I was determined to go. Animists believe everything has a spiritual component—animals, plants, even rocks. This interesting perspective gives everything in existence a new level of meaning. The evening was wonderful, and God used it to teach me a valuable lesson about my attitude. When we arrived at the village, we were gathered together in the village school, a sparse bamboo structure. There wasn't much inside, just some rather rough bamboo benches, with a simple, small bamboo table and a raised bamboo platform at the front of the room. I sat down and was trying to figure out if there was any possible way to be comfortable, when a scruffy looking man arrived. He was dirty and was smoking a cigar, one of my least favorite things, so I prayed that he wouldn't sit near me. The Lord heard my prayer. He sat the man right next to me. Not only did the man not smell bad, but the cigar smoke didn't even bother me. Cigar smoke always makes me nauseous, so I knew that was a miracle. I saw the lesson in this immediately and prayed a prayer of repentance, thanking God for convicting me of a judgmental attitude. But that night was just beginning.

There were ten of us on the team and about sixty local villagers packed into the small, bamboo school. We started by playing a guitar and singing a few worship songs in English, then told the villagers that we had come to spread the Good News about Jesus and what He had done in our lives. Several of us shared our testimonies and then one of the guys on the team asked if anyone wanted to come up front to give their hearts to Jesus.

This was the first time we had ever asked this during the entire trip. It was interesting that the people who came forward were all young. It was a joy to see them accept Jesus as their Savior! We gave a couple more testimonies, and then another guy on the team felt moved to ask the same thing. This time it was the elderly villagers that went forward, and to my surprise, the "scruffy" man that I didn't want to sit next to me was one of them. There was great joy in the room as nine people accepted the Lord that night. It is a night I will never forget. And as for that scruffy man? He was to reappear in my life many more times. The Lord knows how to keep me humble.

Our trip was growing to a close, but the Lord wasn't through with us yet. I went there with the intention of teaching the Karen people about the Lord, but the Lord sent me there to teach me about the Karen people. We were all to learn from this trip. Back in Htee Hta village where we had been staying, we had one last meal cooked and served for us. The team was focused on serving the people, but our Karen hosts insisted on serving us. We didn't want to be treated like guests and be waited on, but our hosts showed us enormous hospitality. They lavished such attention on us that it was actually a bit embarrassing and we were looking for ways to return their kindness. Finally, after our last meal together, we managed to be "successful" in offering some help to our hosts, but it didn't work out the way we planned. It was a simple little act, but it had some significant repercussions. All we did was pick up our dishes together after dinner and carry them to the washing place, rather than leave them for our hosts. When I returned to the simple, wooden house, I heard our host crying in her room. I had no idea what could have happened, so I went in to console her. After asking her several times, she finally stopped crying enough to tell me what the problem was. She told me that by carrying our own plates and not letting them serve us we had deprived them of the only gift they had to give us. I prayed with her and asked her to forgive us. I have never felt so small in my life. I shared this with the team and we were all humbled.

It's not enough to love someone. You need to let them love you back.

The next day it was time to say goodbye to the wonderful people of Htee Hta village and start the journey back home. I hadn't thought anymore about the Lord speaking to me to return to this place. My initial prayer had brought me peace and I felt I needed to do nothing more than wait for the Lord's instruction. We made the long drive back to Bangkok, where we spent the night in a hotel, and the next day our driver took us to the airport. The driver worked for Tribe and Nations Outreach at that time, a small mission organization, and he had a message for me. "The village school headmaster wants you to come back and help at the school."

That took me by surprise. *What can I do in the school? I'm not a teacher. There's no electricity . . . there's no phone . . . there's no typewriter . . . I'm used to working in an office . . . there's nothing in the village. What can I possibly do?*

I expressed my concern to the driver and he told me that they thought I could help by teaching them English. I thought . . . *Well, since I'm an English speaker I might be able to handle that.* I didn't want to neglect the assignment God had given me, so I asked if I could teach English using the Bible as my textbook. They agreed. That sounded promising, so I asked when they wanted me to start. "After the monsoon season," they replied. "Okay," I said, but then had to add, "When is that?" "The end of October or November." We were at the airport, so there wasn't much time for me to think or engage in an extended conversation. "Oh . . . okay," I responded. And that was that. In those few minutes I had agreed to uproot my life, move halfway around the world, and do something I had never done, nor even dreamed of doing. The Lord didn't give me time to overthink this one.

I was a little stunned when I got on the plane, thinking of the enormity of what I had just agreed to do. For the entire flight back to Los Angeles poor Ron Case, who had the bad fortune to be the one sitting next to me, had to listen to a nonstop monologue of my fears and insecurities. "What am I going to do?" "How in the world did I end up in this situation?"

When I wasn't speaking to Ron I was silently praying to the Lord. Neither one of them were giving me any answers at this point. Ron only said he was glad the Lord had called me and not him and that he would do anything for me from America, a promise he has fulfilled to this day, but back then he had no more of an idea what he just committed to than I did. We would have to wait for the Lord to answer.

CHAPTER FOUR

GOD'S CONFIRMATION

Then Jesus said to them, 'Follow Me,
and I will make you become fishers of men.'
Mark 1:17

The Karen Education Department leader was very specific about not wanting me to return until after the monsoon season. He had a good reason: he didn't want me to get malaria and die. The rains and mud can clog the roads, and if I became ill, he would have no way to get me to the hospital. I knew nothing about malaria, other than I was pretty sure I didn't want to get it. I believed that if God sent me there, He would protect me, of course, but there was no point in taking a foolish risk, so I was quite happy to wait six months to avoid it. The school principal and her family were more comfortable with the delay as well, since I would be the first foreigner to ever stay there. It was a big responsibility for them and they wanted to do their best to take care of me.

After a long flight filled with lots of questions, and driving my seat partner, Ron, crazy, we finally landed in Los Angeles. My children picked me up at the airport and we had a happy reunion as they bombarded me with questions about the trip and my experiences. Then my daughter, Shelly, asked a strange question. "So, when are you going back?" The question caught me totally by surprise. "Why did you ask me that?" I asked.

"Because the Lord already told me that you're going back," she replied. *Wow*, I thought. That was the first confirmation that it really was God sending me on this journey. I didn't answer her. Although I had agreed to go back, somehow the invitation just didn't seem real, so I returned to work and settled into my old routine. I would talk to people about the trip from time to time, but returning had a strange feeling of unreality to it. Maybe that's a little coping device our minds put up when we're in denial about something; I don't know. Whatever the cause, I felt okay with the way everything was going and I just moved forward one day at a time.

My coworkers at my office job were wonderful people, but didn't want to hear about my faith, so I couldn't fellowship with them. That was hard for me. I got such strength from being around Christians, and being deprived of Christian fellowship eight hours a day, five days a week, was a bit of a strain. One of the assistant pastors at church knew I would like to have a job with Christians, and he called one day. "There's a job opening for a church school secretary and you would be perfect for it. You should apply for it." Well, I thought that was great. I would love having a job at my church, so I went right down and applied. I went through the usual process that people go through when they apply for a new job, but I wasn't the only applicant. After I went through two interviews, the church narrowed the applicants down to me and one other person. On the next interview the pastor asked me some of the same questions over again. "Why are you still asking me the same questions? I've already given you my answers. They're not going to change." He said to me, "Every time I pray about it, the Lord shows me you're going on the mission field." "Oh . . . that won't be for at least five years, after my kids get married." "Okay," the pastor said, "I'll pray about it again. I'll see what the

Lord says." The Lord spoke to him very clearly that I was going on the mission field, so I didn't get the job. That was the second confirmation that God intended for me to go to Thailand. There was another good part in this story. The woman who got the job was a friend of mine. I wasn't aware that she was the other applicant, but when she got the job, I was very happy for her. God always knows what is best, and I felt a little nudge in my spirit from the Lord.

Around this time, I got a call from Pastor Greg Laurie at Harvest Christian Fellowship, whose church mission team I had been with. He had heard that I might be going back to Thailand as a missionary, so I guess he felt a little bit of responsibility for me. He asked to meet with me to tell him how the Lord was leading me, so I did. Greg pointed out some of the potential problems in missionary work, and he had a big concern that there was no one from my own culture going with me. He knew that Satan would attack me for serving the Lord on the front lines, and that I would need someone to pray with. Greg also asked me to speak at different home Bible studies to ask if anyone felt led by the Lord to accompany me on the trip. No one responded. He also arranged for me to meet with another person, his spiritual mentor, to be sure that this trip was the right thing for me.

As time grew short, events continued to fall into place. One day I took my car in for some work at a Christian mechanic's shop, who also went to Harvest, and in the course of our conversation he asked me if I knew of anyone who had a house available to rent. He and his family had to move out of their current house the next month, but the builders hadn't finished constructing their new house yet. I told him I didn't know of an available place offhand, but I would let him know if I heard anything. As I drove away, I clearly heard the Lord say, "Yes you do." It was true, I wasn't going to need a house in California if I was living in Thailand. I called him later and told him that I could move out of my house at the end of August if he wanted it. He was really excited and said it would work out great for him and his family.

In case I hadn't gotten the message on which direction God wanted me to go yet, He decided to give me a much bigger nudge. The people at work had gotten wind of what was going on in my life, including my boss. Another roofing company in town had gone out of business and their secretary needed a job. My boss figured, since I was probably leaving anyway, she would let me go and hire the secretary. The good news was that the roofing company gave me a month's severance pay and my part of their profit-sharing plan. The bad news was that I was unemployed. Through the four affirmations and confirmations, I finally realized that I would indeed be going to Thailand in a few months. My target departure time would be the end of October 1985.

So, not only did I not have a job, but for two months I wouldn't have a place to live, either. The next Sunday night after church I approached a group from the singles ministry that was talking together after church and asked if anyone could take me in for a couple of months. I got a surprisingly quick response. "Sure, I'll take you in." It was Laurie, a woman I didn't even know. I pointed that out to her, and that it might not work out. She said that was okay, that she knew the Lord wanted her to do it, but was concerned that I hadn't seen her apartment and I might not like it. She decided to take me there to see if I approved. It couldn't have worked out better. My children were all away at college, and the girls living with me through the church lodging ministry found new places to live, so I moved out of my house and the mechanic and his family moved in. My new friend Laurie provided a bedroom with my very own bathroom—something I had never had—and I stayed there for two months. Laurie and I became, and are still, good friends. The Lord arranged everything.

As it turned out, there wasn't time for me to meet with Greg's mentor on the outreach trip we were on, so before I left, the pastors at Harvest prayed for me, anointed me with oil, and sent me with their blessing. Departure day was emotional and full of so many blessings. Many friends came to see me off at the airport and I was filled with such excitement, thankfulness, and joy in the midst of the weird feelings of "What am I going into?!" Those feelings intensified as I left everyone and walked through customs by myself. As soon as the doors closed after going through immigration, I realized how alone I was, and told the Lord, "It's really just you and me now." Reality hit. I don't even remember any of my thoughts during the long flights to Thailand.

The six months that had seemed so long at first were suddenly gone; it was time for my new adventure to begin. The same driver for Tribe and Nations Outreach on our exposure trip met me at the airport, then we flew together to Malaysia, because the roads to the village were still closed from the monsoon storms. What a jolt in plans—the Lord's first lesson in flexibility—and what life would be like with the Karen people.

We were in Butterworth, Malaysia for six weeks. Getting a truck into the village that would be our final destination was impossible, so we had to wait. Looking back, I think it was the Lord's way of getting me accustomed to Asian culture, Asian food, Asian cold showers, and wet Asian toilet seats. (Soon I would get used to not having a toilet seat at all.)

As it turned out, the six-week wait was valuable for another reason. I ended up getting sick with malaria symptoms. Again,

I probably got the symptoms from the malaria prevention medication I was taking. Fortunately, I could get proper treatment in Malaysia and speak to the medical people in English, so I was able to get through the whole thing without too much stress and too many more adjustments. I was staying with Lydia, who spoke English, and her Chinese-Malaysian family, who didn't. She was the treasurer on my exposure trip from church, and we were going back to Htee Hta village together. The driver was Thai-Karen and could speak English, too, so the cross-culture challenges were a bit less overwhelming, and we could at least worship and pray together. Lydia and I prayed a lot together because we were so anxious and excited to get back to the village. It was comforting to know that however different things were going to be I would at least be able to speak with someone in my own language.

By December the roads were open. We flew into Bangkok and on December 19, 1985, drove into the jungle to Htee Hta, the village that the Lord had told me to return to six months before. It was wonderful. The Christmas season always brings joy to the hearts of Christians, but this was the first Christmas that I experienced the joy of being a missionary, bringing the Good News to a people and land that I was just beginning to know. The schools were closed for the holiday break, so we traveled by boat to several different villages nearby and celebrated Christmas with them. Many of us have attended Christmas plays at our churches or children's schools, but I now found myself in a jungle, halfway around the world, watching the villagers celebrate our Savior's birth in an entirely different cultural perspective. I loved it.

We stayed with Lionel and Esther, the village school principal, and her family, who were from Burma, but could speak English, so I didn't immediately have a language dilemma.

They were absolutely wonderful to us and we appreciated their hospitality so much. However, as I was beginning to experience on a regular basis, God had a different plan from what we thought. A situation came up with Lydia and she had to go back home. So, when school started in January 1986, I was on my own.

Throughout December I had been doing a lot of reading about different missionaries in the book *From Jerusalem to Irian Jaya*, as well as doing some very focused Bible study. For a long time, it had been my heart's desire to have nothing else to do except read God's Word and really understand what it says, what it means, who God really is, and how wonderful He is. For the first time I could do exactly that. It was a wonderful blessing and a wonderful answer to my prayers.

There was absolutely no question in my mind that God had sent me here; there had been far too many confirmations for that. What I did question was exactly *what* God called me here to do. More puzzlingly, why had he called *me*, who had no gifts or abilities to function in a Karen jungle village? All around me I saw so many needs that it was heartbreaking. There were medical needs, food needs, clothing needs—I was overwhelmed suddenly being confronted with the level of deprivation that these wonderful people experienced on a daily basis. It brought tears of hurt and frustration to my eyes knowing that everything I could do still wouldn't be enough. I couldn't take care of everyone's problems, resolve the village's issues, and certainly not take care of the entire country. Nevertheless, there was no doubt that God had sent me into this jungle for a reason. It was up to me to discover that reason and follow His will. I decided to come to God in prayer and fasting, asking Him to reveal His plan for me. My host family was not familiar with biblical fasting and it concerned them that I wasn't eating.

I assured them that if God spoke His will to me in less than a week, I would break the fast, but I really felt that I must pray and fast until I learned exactly what it was that He had called me there to do. Naturally, my fast was the exact opposite of my host family's gift of hospitality, an important part of their culture. However, they could clearly see how important this was to me so they tried to be accommodating.

After a week had passed, I still didn't have my answer, but I knew it would not be right to worry my host family any longer. I stopped my fast, much to their relief, and then Esther said to me, "We want you to teach at school today." This was the original plan, of course, but I wasn't any more comfortable with it then than I had been months before when the idea had first been presented. Nothing that had happened in those six months had magically turned me into a teacher. "What do you want me to teach?" I asked a bit warily. "We want you to teach English." I reminded her that I wanted to use the Bible as the text and she agreed I could, but she also insisted that we leave immediately for the school, so the rest of my lesson planning session—if you could call it that—was conducted while we walked there. No more delays in my missionary work. Whatever God wanted me to do, I would start doing it today.

As we walked, I prayed that God would direct me, and He gave me my answer, but only as I arrived at the school. When I walked into that classroom everything was suddenly clear to me. There were six teenage girls there. I instantly knew that God had called me to disciple them, just as I had discipled young women in my home back in California. It's hard to express how excited I was at that moment. Discipleship is my heart. That is what I really enjoy doing. Instantly the questions I had been asking of God were totally and clearly answered. He had given me a ministry that I loved. I was so excited and grateful to Him.

My quickly concocted lesson plan was to introduce myself to these young girls by sharing my life testimony. As I stood before them speaking through an interpreter, the Lord kept telling me to share John 3:3, but that wasn't part of my testimony. In my mind the Lord and I had a little discussion about this. *That's not part of my testimony!* I thought. "Share John 3:3," He responded. It's not easy to speak and have a mental argument with God at the same time, so I gave up the third time. I opened my Bible and read John 3:3. "'Unless you are born again you cannot enter the kingdom of God.' Do you understand what that means?" I asked. They didn't. I explained to them in detail the concept of what it means to be born again and then asked again if they understood. "Yes, we understand," they all said, "we understand."

Good. Now that we all knew exactly what I was talking about I asked the six girls if they were born again. Three said they were and three said they weren't. I asked the three girls who weren't born again if they would like to be, and they said they would, so I very carefully explained what being born again meant three more times to make sure they really understood. I then asked them again if they wanted to be born again and they all said they did. With that we all prayed, and they received Jesus as their Savior. I now understood the Lord's direction in this matter. I couldn't disciple girls who were not really Christians, so confirming their belief was step one and everything else would follow. The experience was exhilarating. I left my first day of teaching with tremendous excitement and relief knowing that I had obeyed the Lord's will, plan, and timing His way. I clearly understood what being obedient to the Lord really meant and the blessings that come along with it.

Obviously, this would be a good time for the enemy to attack. "What do you think you're doing here?" the enemy spoke to my heart a few days later. This was exactly the kind of thing that my pastor, Greg Laurie, had warned me about. Because I had been warned, and because Jesus is my best friend, I had no trouble facing the challenge head-on. "Three people have been saved, so if that's why the Lord sent me here, that was worth coming all the way here for." I remembered Jesus told the demons to go to the pigs, so I did, too. The enemy didn't bother me anymore.

The following months were a whirlwind of teaching and learning for all involved. I was learning the culture of the country, the girls were learning English and the Bible, and my inquisitive interpreter was even learning what it meant to be a Christian. In a curious way I found that the Karen people approached Christianity in the same way many Americans do. They say they are Christians because their parents are Christians, as though Christian faith is hereditary. We all know people who call themselves Christians because they show up in church for an hour on Sunday, or show up only on Christmas and Easter. They identify as Christians without ever having a personal relationship with the Lord, which is so critical. I immediately realized that God had sent me to the Karen people to teach them to not only proclaim Jesus as their Lord and Savior, but to show them how to have a personal loving relationship with Him that is life-changing. This was the ministry He called me to for Him, to show these wonderful people how to really fall in love with Jesus, and for them to understand His love for them. I found true joy in my new commitment and the months rolled by.

Then, it started to rain. The monsoon season was about to be upon us again with all the difficulties it brought.

CHAPTER FIVE

A WOLF IN SHEEP'S CLOTHING

Be sober, be vigilant; because your adversary the devil
walks about like a roaring lion, seeking whom he may devour.
1 Peter 5:8

The monsoon season brings plenty of grief for everyone. Storms could destroy crops and bamboo homes built on stilts, and anyone could get malaria. With the roads impassable due to water and mud, it was very difficult get to a hospital. This presented a serious potential problem for everyone. My hosts were still afraid I would get malaria, and if I did, there was a strong possibility that I could die. The idea of leaving made me sad, but aside from the issues of my own health, my presence in the jungle during the monsoon season would create a great burden of stress on my hosts. God had sent me to help these people, not put another concern in their already difficult lives. I understood that and agreed to leave. They suggested I wait out the monsoon season in Bangkok or some other place in Thailand where I could receive medical attention if I needed it, but if I couldn't be in the village teaching my students, there really wasn't any good reason for me to be in the region at all. On top of that, I was trying to learn the Karen language, which was very difficult for me. If I went to

Bangkok or another city in Thailand, they would be speaking Thai, which I didn't understand, either. Not only would I not be helping the people God sent me to serve but I would be seriously complicating my own life. If I couldn't be with my students in the village, I thought I might as well go back to the States, so that's what I did.

The timing of my return worked out well. I heard that a group called Survival was conducting a missionary training class, and that was exactly what I needed. I never had any formal missionary training, I just leapt right into obeying God with practically no preparation, so the idea of having some formal training was exciting to me. I joined the class and was not disappointed at all. In fact, in addition to the wonderful training, I enjoyed the whole experience. Just when everything seemed to be going very well, some opposition crept up. There were people who didn't want me to go back to the Karen. It seemed strange that people would want to interfere with the ministry the Lord called me to, but other people recognized that at its source, this was really a spiritual attack. The enemy knew more would give their lives to Jesus, and was trying to stop me. Fortunately, I had good friends giving me good counsel and support. In about six months I was on a plane heading back to the Karen.

The language barrier in Thailand and Burma was an enormous obstacle for me. There was so much in my heart that I wanted to say, but I literally did not have the words. Before I left on my return trip to the States, I found a book that I was hopeful would help me learn the language before I went back. I was optimistic and studied the book diligently, but I have to admit the whole thing was too much for me. The Karen language is very, very different from English. They use sounds—five tones—to form words. You can't learn that from a book.

It was overwhelming and impossible for me, so when I went back, I was very discouraged, but did the best I could. I learned to say "Jesus loves you" in Karen, which is all the same tone, so I could at least walk around the village spreading that message. It was a start. Unfortunately, it was not the only start.

Up to this point my biggest hindrances had been the weather and the languages, but this trip was the start of suspicion and opposition from the villagers. Early on I had never considered that might happen. After all, the village school leaders invited me to help them. Who could object to that? I discovered that just because it was clear in my mind that God had called me, it did not mean it was clear in everyone's mind. My host family explained it to me. We were in a war zone and many of the villagers thought I was a spy. Although that thought seemed ridiculous to me, it made perfect sense to them. They lived in constant fear under Burmese threats and violence. They had to be exceptionally careful in whom they placed their trust. They only trusted the people they had grown up with. I was a stranger, an outsider, and that made me a potential enemy. The fact that my host family obviously trusted me and allowed me to live with them gave me a bit of credibility, but I could see that it might be a long time before the villagers were completely open with me.

That was just the first problem; a second was about to arrive. I had continued my teaching and discipling of a new class, when another missionary arrived and introduced himself. He was from Australia and had begun coming to this area about the same time I did, through the same person that brought me. I was not aware of it, but there is a thing on the mission field called "territorial." Basically, many missionaries work with a group of people, claim that area as their territory, and expect other missionaries to stay away. I had never heard of it before and still don't see it in the Bible, yet here was this Australian missionary telling the school leaders that he did not want me here and I should leave. I didn't have an immediate response for him, so I just listened and silently prayed for God's direction and will. After hearing this, I sought counsel of the village pastor and judge. They told me to stay and keep on obeying the Lord, doing what He called me to do. I remained firm. The Australian would come for a short time, sometimes with teams, then go back to Australia. Everything was fine when he was gone, but when he returned, he continued to stir up trouble and cause division. As it unfolded, I saw that this was a problem that was going to be around for a while.

The next monsoon season I went back to the United States again, just in time for a happy occasion. My second daughter, Shelly, got married. The next year, also during monsoon season, my oldest daughter, Kelly, got married. Before she got married, Kelly came over to visit me. She stayed for a week in the village of Htee Hta; she absolutely loved it and said she would like to come back and live there forever. We really had a great time.

After their wedding she decided to come with her husband, Dave, so I headed back to Thailand to get things ready for their arrival. Unfortunately, the Australian had not been sitting idle while I was gone. He had been working together with the Thai-Karen driver from the Tribes and Nations Outreach who had taken me to the village in the beginning. Shortly after returning to Bangkok, I received a call from the Thai-Karen who said, "You need to leave Thailand and go back to the US. You have no business being here." All I could think of was, "What is Your will, Lord?" I only wanted to do what He wanted me to do and that was going to take some discernment on my part. I knew that responding strictly from my flesh would only bring destruction on the Lord's ministry to the Karen, not the blessings of God's truth and love that I had come to spread, so I only told the Thai-Karen I that I would pray to see what God wanted me to do.

For the next two months I stayed in Bangkok just sitting at the Lord's feet asking, "What do *You* want me to do? Not what this person wants me to do but what do *You* want me to do, Lord?" As I prayed and sought His will in the Bible, and got counsel from other Christians who knew the situation, I got a very strong sense for what He wanted me to do: He wanted me to go back to the village. This was confirmed shortly thereafter. In God's perfect timing, the person who invited me to go in the beginning, Lionel, the education department leader, came to me and said, "I'm taking you back to the village this is ridiculous . . . this is nonsense." I felt great relief that God's will was being restored. We waited for my daughter and son-in-law to arrive, then we all went to the village together.

The rainy season was longer than usual that year and back in full force with all of the associated complications. It was hard enough on the villagers, although they were used to it and prepared to deal with it, but for those of us who were less experienced and trying to travel through the downpours it was a big, soggy, muddy nightmare. All the dirt roads were flooded including the one to our village, which meant we had to leave the relative comfort of our truck and finish our journey on foot. This involved wading across thirty-six small rivers (I counted them).

Without the truck we could only take what we could carry, and that meant we could only take the things that were absolutely necessary. My son-in-law Dave took his guitar, my daughter took her camera, and I carried some of their clothes, because my clothes were already in the village. Despite the brutal and sometimes harrowing trek, we managed to make it to the village with everything except one shoe. Dave got one of his feet stuck in the mud crossing a river and it pulled his flip flop off. It was caught up in the fast-flowing water never to be seen again. Considering all of the things that could have gone wrong, losing one flip flop wasn't all that bad, although his feet were so much bigger than the typical Asian man's that it was hard for him to find new ones.

While I was gone, the villagers worked together to build a bamboo house with a wooden floor for me. The funding was provided by a visiting nurse from Australia. My hosts had all been kind, but having a place of my own where I could study and have others over was something I was really looking forward to. When we arrived at the village, there it was. Sort of. They had worked very diligently, but they had run out of money, so they only completed half of a house. Nevertheless, it was built with love and it was dry. We put our few belongings in the upstairs rooms and were grateful for what we had. Unfortunately, one of the more modern conveniences had not been built yet when the money ran out. We didn't have a bathroom. For that particular necessity we were going to have to use the bush beside the house. It wasn't the first time, and it certainly wouldn't be the last. Being a missionary rarely comes with all the conveniences of home.

My Karen children came from other villages, and occasionally, a stray family member came into the fold as well. At that time, the youngest Karen child the Lord gave me was separated from his mother due to some harsh circumstances. His mother was in prison. I was teaching a Bible course in the women's prison and my first meeting with the woman was memorable, to put it mildly. She almost scared me. Her skin color was very dark, almost black, and she was about as hard-looking a person as I have ever seen. I went every Sunday with an interpreter, so I asked her if she knew who Jesus Christ was and she said no, that she had never heard of Him. I said, "Well I'm going to teach about who He is now. Would like to hear about Him?" "No," she replied. I said, "Okay. Then you can go sit in the corner. You don't have to listen." It was one big bamboo room where all the women slept. She went over and sat in the corner and I continued to have the Bible study. The next Sunday she asked if she could join in and listen with the others. I said, "Sure." It took about a year, but during that year I saw her whole countenance change. She just softened and glowed. I was marveling that she was enjoying the Bible study.

One day, while I was in my home in Htee Hta village, the Lord spoke to me and said, "Go to the women's prison." I thought that was strange, but it was very clear to me. I went to get my colleague, Daniel Zu, and said, "I don't know why, but the Lord wants me to go to the women's prison. Can you please go with me to translate for me?" He agreed, so we headed there. We were required to go across the dirt road to the men's side first to get permission from the prison authorities to see her. When we arrived there the guard said, "I'm so glad you're here! Boo Shree Moo is waiting in the office for you." That was the last thing I was expecting to hear, and I asked the guard why she wanted to see me. He didn't know, but told us that she told him we were coming and asked if she could wait in the prison office for us. How did she know we were coming? There are no phones in the village, and I had not talked to anybody.

It was becoming clear to me that God was behind this. Daniel and I looked at each other in amazement, then walked in to the office. She greeted us with obvious happiness. "I'm so glad you're here. I knew you would come. I've been waiting for you." "Great!" I said, "Why?" "Well, I want to accept Jesus Christ as my Lord and Savior." Daniel and I looked at each other again in amazement and were really excited. Not being entirely certain how much she had picked up from the class, we explained to her what salvation is all about. In that forlorn, dismal prison, she confirmed that she wanted to be saved. She prayed and accepted Jesus as her Lord and Savior. These are the moments that make the trials of being a missionary more than worthwhile. Later, she asked if I would teach her son, Saw Po Rah, about Jesus and send him to school.

I was so excited, but needed to talk to the village leaders about the plan for him, so I went to the village judge. He not only totally approved, he arranged for an outboard motor canoe and driver to take me there to get him. Boo Shree Moo was released from jail and back in her village then, but it was far away from the village at the riverbank and too far for me to walk. They sent villagers to bring her son to me. I loved him the minute I saw him. His mom and some of her family came with him. They had him sleep next to me that night, with one of the others singing Karen poetry late into the night. I could tell it was from their religion of animism, the belief that a supernatural power in nature animates the universe, so I kept quiet and prayed for him.

As we were getting in the boat to go back to Htee Hta village, he started crying and didn't want to leave. His mom began promising him many things to get him to go, even that I would take him to America. I didn't understand what she was saying, but I understood "America," so I prayed for wisdom. I realized he was afraid he wasn't ever coming back and would never see his mom or family again, so I told him he would be back during school break. As soon as he knew he was coming back, he got in the boat and we were on our way. I don't remember much of the two-day boat trip back because I didn't understand the language, so I just kept praying for him.

He was quite the sensation when we arrived. He was Karen, but didn't look like the other children because he had long hair, and was wearing earrings, a bracelet, and a necklace, all made from strings. These were part of the animist culture in his home village, but in Htee Hta, the villagers all thought he was a girl as we walked down the village road. He loved walking with me and asked how to say things in English like star and sun. The girls living with me—I had four from Bla Oh Hta village by then—all began taking care of him, slowly removing his "jewelry" one piece at a time. He was doing okay, but early one morning I heard him crying. I thought it was something that would pass quickly, but when it didn't, I went to get Daniel Zu to interpret for me. When Daniel and I returned and saw him, I understood the problem immediately. They had cut his hair! That was going way too far for him. He looked nothing like when he arrived, and he wasn't all that happy about having his entire identity changed. Daniel Zu was wonderful, as always, and told him how handsome he was with his new look. He also explained that now the villagers recognized that he was a boy. I am sure that made a difference.

It would have been great if the cultural challenges of the area were nothing more complex than grooming, but haircuts were the least of our problems. The culture of the country and of the Karen people was bound in the context of a seemingly endless war. During this period in Htee Hta we dug trenches in the ground, because we heard that airplanes were going to come over and bomb us. Despite the danger, I felt great peace if I had to go into a trench. At that time, Saw Po Rah was in the hospital with asthma and malaria, and he was anemic. He was too sick to care for at home, so every day I walked to the hospital on the open, dirt road, fifteen minutes each way, because he needed to be ministered to and taken care of. Travelling in the open was dangerous in those days, but it had to be done. Two of my girls stayed with him at night at the hospital, then I went to help him during the day while they were at school.

Each time danger was announced, I had peace. I knew I was where the Lord wanted me to be, so I was obedient and I stayed. Others may have different ideas, but that is how I believe the Lord has called me. Ironically, I am afraid of needles, but I was never afraid of the Burmese Army. That has to be the Lord. I mean, I am not a person who relishes pain—I suppose no one does—but I have a very low pain threshold. The thought of a needle being stuck into my body absolutely unnerves me, but the thought of the Burmese coming, well, I just had peace. I was actually excited that if they came, I would be able to share the Gospel with them. I had Burmese language Christian tracts with me, and when we fled in 1997, I left them all over the school compound. My prayer was when the Burmese troops arrived, they would read them and would come to know the love, the truth, and the Gospel of Jesus Christ, who died for them and loves them. I pray that God used those tracts.

When we fled in 1997, I prayed for God's direction and He showed me not to go out the same way we had fled previously. Again, He gave me total peace through Psalm 32:8-10: "I will instruct you and teach you in the way which you should go. I will counsel you with My eye upon you." Many are the sorrows of the wicked, but he who trusts in the Lord, loving kindness shall surround him." Also, Psalm 118:17, "I will not die but live, and tell the works of the Lord." Again, He gave me His total peace.

While we fled by the river, Saw Po Rah got off the boat at his village. His mother wanted him to come and help her flee, which I totally understood. I didn't see him again until he arrived at the refugee camp where I was helping. I was arranging for several of my children to go to another refugee camp up north, and asked him if he wanted to go because he could continue to go to school there. He agreed, so he went with the others, finished high school there, and went on to graduate from the Bible school there.

This happened many times when I was in the village. It is quiet there. There aren't the distractions of a city. It's really a blessing to be able to be in a quiet place and hear the Lord's voice. On one occasion the Lord told me to go to the hospital. So again, I got Daniel and said, "He wants me to go to the hospital. Can you go with me?" As always, he said yes and off we went. As in the case of the prison, we didn't know who the Lord wanted us to see, so we just went from person to person, knowing he would lead us when the time was right. We ended up spending much of our time with one particular family, talking and sharing the Gospel. They had two little children, one of whom was very sick and hospitalized. As they waited for news about their child, they listened to us intently and asked questions.

The Good News of salvation sounds wonderful, but making the lifestyle changes that go with it can be hard, and that was the problem the husband was having. As we talked about the Christian life, he would say things like "Well, I'm not willing to give up my drinking. I'm not willing to give up my smoking. I'm not willing to give up my beetle nut. I had a wife before who died, she wanted me to become a Christian, now this one wants me to become a Christian, but I don't want to give up my old life." Questioning the wife, we quickly discovered that she was not a Christian, either. She wanted to become one, but she wouldn't unless her husband joined her in that commitment of faith.

The Bible tells us that we should not be unequally yoked. In other words, believers should marry believers so that an unbelieving spouse can't destroy the mate's faith. I am certainly in favor of that, having personally gone through the trials of trying to enjoy Christian life with an unbelieving husband. However, we didn't appear to be getting anywhere. The wife wanted to be a Christian but wouldn't do it unless her husband joined her, and the husband wasn't going to join her if it meant giving up his bad habits. We appeared to be stuck. You can't—and shouldn't—try to force Christianity on anyone. Daniel and I had been speaking with this couple for forty-five minutes and gotten nothing but excuses from the husband.

We were tired. We were getting nowhere. Daniel and I turned to each other with looks of resignation, and decided to end the visit. We excused ourselves and began to leave, when the husband said, "Aren't you going to pray for me?" We looked at each other, looked at him, and asked, "What would you like us to pray for?" He said, "I want to accept the Lord, and so does my wife." Both Daniel and I felt bad that we almost walked away without completing the Lord's work. We were sensitive enough to hear Him say, "Go to the hospital," but not what He wanted us to do when we got there. We stayed, prayed with them, and they accepted the Lord. I didn't know it then, but this man is the father of Bah Bluit Moo, one of the village school students. He is also the scruffy man I had prayed to the Lord for him to not sit near me when I came on the team. The Lord continues to humble me.

It was their son, Bah Bluit Moo, who was hospitalized. He was in high school at this time and struggling from really bad headaches. A visitor arrived from Singapore, and I told him about Bah Bluit Moo. I asked him if we could go over to the boy's dorm and pray for him. He agreed, and when he found

Bah Bluit Moo, he noticed he was wearing something around his neck and asked him where it came from. He said a friend had given it to him. My friend believed the neckwear was symbolic of superstition and false religion, so he asked him if he would be willing to take it off. He took it off, we prayed for him, and his headaches were gone.

Not long after, I saw him sharing at a youth service at the village church and he was so spirit-filled he was almost glowing. I asked him afterward what he wanted to do after he graduated from high school the next year, and he said he would like to go to Bible school. In that part of the world nothing, including going to school, is easy, but I made the commitment to help him. "You can go," I said. "We'll figure it out somehow," and we did. We were able to send him to the Bible school in Beh Klaw refugee camp, where he got the education he was longing for. Unfortunately, that was also the place where he had a stroke. Satan may slow us down, but he doesn't stop us. After being hospitalized, going through rehabilitation at McKean Hospital, and graduating from Bible School, Bah Bluit Moo went to Tham Hin refugee camp where he became the pastor of his own church. We never know why God leads us to the people He leads us to. I just love watching His big plan unfold. He has a reason for everything He asks us to do, and for going to every place He asks us to go. I am in awe as I see all the puzzle pieces come together to fulfill His great plan, and His great commission. I am honored and blessed to be one of those pieces.

By this time, near the end of October, 1988, one of my former students, Friday, had graduated from high school and was a teacher at Htee Hta school. She moved into the house with us to help us—my eldest daughter, her husband, and me—with the cooking, washing, and our daily practical needs while we were teaching. This was a big help in so many ways. I was still struggling to learn the Karen language, which made even some of the smallest things more complicated to do. Having help was a literal godsend.

As Christians, we always look forward to Christmas when we celebrate the birth of our Savior Jesus Christ. Even on the other side of the world from my California birthplace, in the jungles along the Thai-Burma border, people celebrate this as a time of peace and joy. There is a two-week break in the schools, and villagers from the Christian churches go Christmas caroling from village to village. It's beautiful, uplifting, and exciting, but Christmas 1988 had an extra component. While I was out caroling with the villagers, the Australian and the Thai-Karen driver came back into the village and started spreading lies and rumors to cause division among the people the Lord had sent me to serve. My daughter and son-in-law were with me, so I had a great deal of emotional support; nevertheless, I have to admit I was in a state of shock. Why were these people believing these things? When I would see the Australian, he would look me straight in the eyes and say, "God bless you. I'm glad you're here," but behind my back he was spreading terrible lies. He told people that I really wasn't doing anything productive, that I just lay around sleeping and eating the rice that had been provided for the starving children.

Those who saw me on a daily basis knew that I was teaching in the village school every day, had a Bible study at the women's prison on Sundays, and paid for all of my own food. Those people weren't my concern. It was the people who didn't have daily contact with me who could be susceptible to believing these attacks on me. That was upsetting. To make the situation even worse, the Australian was a missionary and a pastor. He was supposed to be serving the Lord, doing what was best for the people, and he was certainly supposed to be telling the truth. This was a case of the "wolf in sheep's clothing." This man was not serving God, and if you're not serving God, you know who you *are* serving. There's only one other choice. These personal attacks on me were hurtful, but worst of all, they had the potential to disrupt the work that I knew God had sent me to do. I had my share of spiritual battles on the mission field, but this one was one of the worst. I needed someone to talk to.

In any situation, prayer is always my first step. God responds in many ways, one of which is to put people in our lives who we can trust to give us comfort and good counsel. In this situation I went to the people God had put in my life to support me. The first was the village pastor. Christians, even Christian leaders, (or maybe, especially Christian leaders) need someone to whom they are accountable. Regardless of our commitment to serve the Lord, we are still human and have human frailties. We need someone to provide good counsel, and I had made myself accountable to the village pastor, Pastor Moses. The other person I sought out at this time was the village judge. The pastor and the judge had both shown a commitment to support me and to do what was best for the villagers, so there was a little bit of peace just being in their presence.

They both gave me the same advice: continue to obey the Lord. Don't think about anything else. Don't think about what they're saying. In other words, they encouraged me to follow God's direction which He had so clearly given me, and not allow the enemy to upset me and wear me down. This is easier said than done, of course, but that's another part of our human frailty. Relying on God is God's way. The road may still be bumpy, but the outcome is sure. Dave and Kelly were a great encouragement to me during this emotionally trying time. They compared my situation to that of Joseph. I was in the bottom of the pit, and there was a time I would come out of this pit, and would be able to go forward. It was a pretty good comparison, since I certainly felt like I was in a pit, and the reminder that God would not leave me there gave me strength.

The attacks by the Australian were relentless. Eventually he said that as long as I was there, he would not help that village anymore. This presented a problem for the villagers, since the Australian had money and I didn't. I came to give my time and my love to the Karen people. As far as money went, I had just enough to go out and renew my visa every three months. The Australian had money and was able to provide many things for the villagers. He could buy things like water pumps that were desperately needed, as well as other things to make the quality of their lives better. We take things like tap water for granted, but in many places it's a luxury. It is completely understandable that the villagers would want the things the Australian could provide and be very hesitant to do something that would cause him to leave. I had absolutely no way of responding at an economic level. What a blessing to everyone it would have been if we could have worked together, but that was not in the Australian's plan. I just stayed quiet, observed, prayed, read the Bible, and waited on the Lord.

The Lord didn't provide me with a great deal of money, but he gave me other gifts of a different value: wisdom and discernment. Knowing this, I try to be patient as He leads me where He wants me to go. The previous year, before my house was built, I was reading a book in my bedroom. I suddenly felt the Holy Spirit say to me, "Go out and ask what the women in the front room of the house are talking about." I looked out the door and one of them was Esther, my host and the village school principal, so I went out, and asked, "What are you two talking about?" She responded, "She is telling me about her daughter who wants to go to school, and has cried for three years because she can't go." I followed up with more questions and learned that the family didn't have the money to provide her with an education. I asked how much it cost to go to school, and she told me it was sixty dollars a year. That certainly didn't strike me as an unsurmountable amount, so I decided that on my next trip to the States I would work and earn the sixty dollars for this poor child who has cried for so many years to go to school. When I told them that, the mother said, "Well, she has a sister, too." "How many sisters?" I asked cautiously. "Only one." *Okay*, I thought, *one hundred twenty dollars. Still not insurmountable. If I can earn sixty, I can earn one hundred twenty.* "Tell her to tell the girls to come to school next year." She was really excited. What seems like such a small thing to us was life-changing to her.

The sisters came and stayed in the girls' dorm until I had my own place, but when they arrived it seemed to rile the Australian and his opposition increased dramatically. His threats to cut his support became a real concern to Esther. She decided to take me out of teaching at the village school so the Australian would continue his financial help. The children were living with me then, and I was in shock. I couldn't talk to them because of the language barrier, so I prayed fervently, asking God what He wanted me to do. Then, again, I went to the village pastor and judge for advice. They were both adamant that I should stay on the course that God had sent me on and not back down. Okay, but what should I be doing? The principal of the school advised me to focus on the Bible study I was teaching at the women's prison. All of a sudden, I realized that I had time to study the Karen language now. This break in teaching could be an opportunity in disguise.

Not long before, I had received the one and only Karen

language lesson book that had been written, by a missionary, Emilie Ballard. (You will read a bit later how the Lord miraculously arranged this.) I had tried many ways to learn the Karen language, including enrolling in kindergarten. I couldn't keep up with the little ones because they had already learned the alphabet before they started school. (God has His ways of keeping us humble.) Fortunately, the kindergarten teacher took pity on me and became my Karen language tutor. I studied from 7:00 a.m. until 7:00 p.m., when it got dark. All day, every day. The only thing I did for ministry was continue at the women's prison on Sundays. The principal of the school told me she believed that was my main ministry anyway. God had now arranged it so I could study the Karen language and teach the women in prison the Bible at the same time. I really had a burden for them. I was very happy with the whole situation. It reminded me of Genesis 50, when Joseph told his brothers that they meant it for evil, but God meant it for good. I felt like that was what was happening with the Australian, that he meant it for evil, but God meant it for good. It turned out to be a blessing.

I worked so hard to learn to speak Karen, and I had such meager results, that it became an emotional drain. At one point I thought I would go back to the States—that I had heard the Lord wrong—that if He had really called me, He would enable me to learn the language. I was beginning to pack my things when Pastor Moses came over to visit. He saw my belongings laid out alongside my luggage and asked what I was doing. I told him what I was thinking and he said, "No, no, no, you cannot leave." Then he told me a story about a missionary in India who had been there for ten years and couldn't learn the language. As I was doing, the Indian missionary was packing his bags when all the people he had been ministering to surrounded him and wouldn't let him leave. The missionary said, "But I can't speak your language." And they said, "You don't need to . . . we know that you love us, and that's what's important. We don't want you to leave." Pastor Moses continued, "We know that you love us, and that's what counts more than anything else." It was extremely humbling. I could only respond, "Okay." I stopped packing my bags.

There is a lesson here, of course. When we experience setbacks or failure, Satan sees our weakness and whispers discouragement in our ear. We are all susceptible to his attacks, but God is also watching. He steps in and is faithful to continue to encourage us, as He did to me at this time. He sent Pastor Moses to deliver His message, and he delivered it well. I must set aside my feelings of inadequacy and continue to stay and minister to the Karen people. Because it's God's will, and because I love them.

Pastor Moses continued to encourage me by inviting me to go to a Karen Pastors' Conference up north. As always, the journey was an adventure. We started with a group of us piling into a big ten-wheel truck in the middle of the night. We traveled over the bumpy jungle roads in the darkness, then came to a border crossing. From there it got more challenging. We had to travel through the jungle for about a week, sometimes by foot, sometimes by ox cart. We stayed in huts along the way each night. After what seemed like an eternity, we arrived at our final destination. I had no idea where I was. I still could not speak Karen, but I enjoyed fellowship with whoever could speak some English. One pastor decided it was God's will for me to live and minister in his village. After praying and talking to Pastor Moses, we both agreed it was not God's will. Aside from the help in clarifying God's plan for me, it was enormously encouraging to hear Pastor Moses say he believed it was still God's will for me to minister in Htee Hta village.

At the conference I met a Karen lady who could speak English and told her of my difficulties learning the Karen language. I asked her for advice and she told me to meet with her husband in Chiang Mai. Perhaps he could help me. His ministry was teaching the Bible by extension and he was good in English. Immediately after the conference I found my way to Chiang Mai instead of going back to Htee Hta village. The only suggestion he had to help me was to direct me to Emilie Ballard, the only one who had written a Karen language book. He told me she lived in Kanchanaburi—the closest town to Htee Hta village! I had been traveling through this town and back every three months for three years to renew my visa and didn't know anything about her or her book. I was so excited. I left for Kanchanaburi immediately, but had no idea how to find her once I arrived. I had no address or phone number, only her name. But, as always, God is in control. When I stepped off the bus, I noticed a white-skinned lady standing among the brown-skinned crowd, looking around like she was waiting for someone. I waited for a while, then asked her if she knew of Emilie Ballard. She did. In fact, she *was* Emilie Ballard. Talk about God directing my steps. The visitor she was waiting for didn't arrive, so she said God must have meant for her to meet me. She took me to her home and gave me the only copy of her book she had left. I immediately headed back to Htee Hta to finally start learning the language.

One of the more common metaphors in Christianity is that of the believer as clay in the hands of God, the potter who shapes us. Nonbelievers may not understand, but it is so true. The most wonderful thing that the Lord was teaching me was to totally die to self . . . to set the desires of my own flesh aside and allow God to create in me the person he wanted me to be. When I first arrived at Htee Hta village there was no phone, no transportation, no newspaper, nothing that I was familiar with anywhere. I was totally at the mercy of the Karen people and God. I could not organize or do anything. I had to change languages, food, clothing, thinking, bathing in the river, going to the toilet, (which could be a hole in the ground—they were all squat potties—or there frequently was no potty at all, I just used the bush). Everything was different. Absolutely *everything*. I had to totally die to self, and not think American anymore. That really helped and brought me so close to the Lord— because He was in control I didn't have to be.

Just because God is directing our paths, it doesn't mean it's going to be the easiest one. I remember one time when two friends came over from the US. I had to walk to the next village, wait for a truck, get on it, ride to Bangkok, and meet them at the airport. The walk was five hours and the truck ride was over three hours. The truck brought us back to the village and they were there for three days. The day they were supposed to leave they asked what time the truck would arrive to pick them up. I told them I didn't know when it would come, just that it would come eventually. Their answer was typical: "What do you mean you don't know?!" They were starting to panic and went into the room to pray. I just smiled because God had been faithful in absolutely everything—100 percent—so I knew He was going to bring the truck in time. It was hard to explain to them, because unlike in the States, life here is not controlled by the clock. At the time there was only one truck among all the Karen villages and, of course, there were many reasons that it had to be used. The truck showed up within an hour and they were praising the Lord for answering their prayers. It was really neat for them to see the Lord's faithfulness, and how He provides everything that we need.

Kelly and Dave stayed until near the end of the school

year teaching English, then returned to the US. They had been a tremendous source of love and support and I was grateful that they had stayed with me that long. My pastor in America wanted me to return every year and share at the church so people wouldn't forget me and my grandchildren would know me. It turned out, as I look back, I could see a pattern. Even if my pastor hadn't called me back, the Lord would have led me to go back. It was usually one of my children getting married, or having a baby, or needing help. So, from 1985 to 2019, even though it made me tired, I went back to the States every year. However, the Lord led me to not return in 2020. I was seventy-eight years old by then and the long flights to get to the US and back, plus the many flights I needed to take when I got there to see all of my children, who had moved to different states, was taking its toll on me. At least I thought that was why He led me to not return. It turned out that was the year of the COVID-19 virus and I couldn't have traveled anyway. He really does know everything beyond a shadow of doubt. But it was a blessing to return every year for thirty-three years because I was able to have a relationship with my grandchildren, and great-grandchildren as they were growing up, and I praise the Lord for that.

By the time they finished building my house in Htee Hta village, a pastor from another village came to me and asked me if I would be interested in building a Christian school. Of course, that would be my heart's desire! The village school, where I had been teaching, was a government school. There was prayer time in the morning and before the Australian's interference, I was teaching the Bible, but that was it. I was really excited about the idea of building a Christian school where I would be able to focus more on the Lord, teach the Bible, and disciple the students. There was the usual problem: I did not have any money. I received fifty dollars a month from my supporters, but every three months I had to leave the country to renew my visa, and that cost fifty dollars. I told him I could pray. Apparently, he had been hoping for something a little more tangible than prayer. He seemed a bit discouraged that that was all I was going to do, but the Lord had shown me time and time again that when I take my needs and desires to Him, He will always bring the right outcome.

I didn't have to wait too long; it was time to renew my visa. I was required to leave Thailand every three months to do so, and that was an adventure in itself. Each time I would have to leave the school, walk five hours to the next village carrying a backpack, find a truck, get to the nearest city, take a bus to Bangkok, buy a train ticket, and go out of the country. (You can get an awful lot of exercise as a missionary.) I always went to Malaysia because it was the closest and they spoke English. I guess God really wanted this school built, because out of the blue, with no connection to the pastor, I got a letter right before one of these trips asking me to come down to Singapore. Somebody down there wanted to meet me about building a Christian school. I thought, *Wow, That's exciting!* I called, and they said that they would meet me at the train station. I got on the train and it took two days to get from Thailand to Singapore through Malaysia. I didn't know who was meeting me, but when I arrived at the train station, I heard my name called, so I followed them and they took me to the office of the man who was interested in helping build the school. This seems to be his ministry. He likes buying land and building things. We talked and he agreed that he would help build the school by sending payments in three installments. I came back with the news that we had the funding to start building the school.

Our governor and others started looking for the right

village to build it in and decided on a village called Ah Moe. The building financing was structured over three payments, so we started construction there as soon as we received the first installment. It was exciting watching this school going up, knowing it would be an evangelism tool that anyone could come to and we would share the Gospel with all of them. I was really excited about this.

Just when things were looking so good, the Australian returned and was not at all pleased to find out what was happening. He was friendly to my face, but he was very busy behind my back, which I discovered the next time I went out to renew my visa. The next financial installment for the school construction was due at this time and it wasn't there. I was completely bewildered. Everything had been going so well and the funder seemed sincere and committed to financing the construction. What could have gone wrong? The Lord, in His faithfulness, gave me the answer and a lot more. While I was still trying to understand all of this, I went to have a meal at a restaurant in Bangkok, which is a huge city, like New York or Los Angeles. While I was sitting there eating, a Karen friend of mine, who lived twelve hours away in Chiang Mai, came into that same restaurant with his wife. I'm not a mathematician, but it's quite easy to see that the odds of that happening by chance are pretty much nonexistent. The Lord was at work again.

When my Karen friend saw me, he came over and said, "I am so sorry to hear what is happening to you." I said, "Please explain to me, what is happening to me?" He said, "Don't you know that an Australian went down to Singapore and talked against you and stopped everything?" I responded that I had no idea what was going on. I was completely in the dark. He continued, "He went down and talked to the donor and told him all you do is eat and sleep, and it would be useless to help you because there are only ten houses in Ah Moe village. It would be a waste of money, so he didn't need to help you, he needed to help him, the Australian, and the things he wanted to do." I was stunned by the news, but also amazed at the way I received the information. I thought, *God is so faithful, and has His ways of letting me know what's going on.*

I finished my meal, and called the office in Singapore. The donor was out of the country. He was in Australia, and the secretary didn't know anything, except he wouldn't be back soon. This was a huge setback and I really didn't know what else to do, so I went back to the village and told the pastor, whose vision it was to build this school, what had happened. "I guess we're just not going to get any more money," I told him sadly. "We'll have to make it smaller, simpler, or make some adjustments." He seemed quite disappointed. I thought there was nothing I could do, so once again I prayed and trusted the Lord for the outcome.

Shortly after that, a person came from Singapore to Htee Hta village to see me and said the donor wanted me to go out of the village to a telephone and call him. I was excited about straightening out this whole situation, but when I called him, it really didn't help. He was discouraging over the phone, saying that it wasn't worth helping me build the school, and his negative comments went on and on. Fortunately, the person who came from Singapore didn't give up any easier than I do. He decided that I needed to resolve this situation with the donor face-to-face, so he convinced the donor to provide me the funds for another trip to meet him again in Singapore. I knew this man had been fed lies and I wanted to counter them with the truth. When I saw him in person, I spoke straight to him, "I believe this is God's school," I told him, "I believe that He will finish what He has started. If you don't want to be part of finishing it, that's okay. If you want to believe this man who can talk smoothly, and is a charmer, that's okay. That's your choice. But I'm a straight talker, and I tell the truth. I'm not going to try to charm you or try to say nice things to you. I don't even know how to do that. I don't believe I have to beg for money for something that I believe is God's will. I just want you to pray about it, then let me know what your answer is."

The next day he called me into his office, and said, "Okay, I will continue helping you build the school." "Praise the Lord!" I went back to Thailand, took the money out of the bank, and went back to the village with the second installment for the school. There have been so many instances like that throughout my time with the Karen—there are so many spiritual battles— yet the Lord shows Himself faithful through every single one. Usually, they were spiritual battles against me personally. Somehow the Lord always gets me through these, and I realize it doesn't matter what other people think. It's only what God thinks that matters. If He knows that I'm being obedient, if I'm listening to Him, and doing what He wants me to do, and I'm pleasing Him, that's the bottom line. That's really what matters.

With our funding finally secured permanently we were able to complete construction of the Christian school and open it for classes in June 1991. It was a joyous occasion. Our troubles weren't entirely over, but there were many good times to offset the painful ones. Most of the painful trials came from the Australian who continued to try to drive a wedge between us and the donor, although he was unsuccessful. We even had a little opposition among the Karen people that had its origins in jealousy, who were speaking out against us. Still, we were able to teach there in relative safety for years. We were still in a war zone, of course, and we had to flee for three months in 1995, when the Burmese Army attacked nearby, but for the most part we lived in peace.

With Ah Moe Mission School completed, I had one less worry on my mind and could focus more on my primary mission, which was bringing the Gospel to the Karen people and discipling. One of the most exciting things for me during this period was helping with another weakness among the Karen, evangelism. Most were very receptive to hearing the Word, but less willing to spread it. Every December they celebrated Jesus' birthday the whole month, but they tended to focus on the celebration more so than the reason for the celebration. They would have secular Christmas celebrations, much like we have in the United States, or go Christmas caroling from village to village, but that would be the extent of their celebrations. This began to change with help from Youth With A Mission Far East Evangelism Teams (YWAM FEET). They came over two different times and taught our students to perform dramas about Jesus' birth, crucifixion, and resurrection, how to stay away from the sins of the world, and how to live as Christians. The Karen are extremely talented and creative. They learned those dramas within the week the teams were there. The YWAM people were amazed. They said it took them six months to learn these things, but the Karen could learn the dramas and the songs in a week. It was the Lord's anointing. It was wonderful. We finally had a real evangelism team in place.

The first year that we planned to go downriver to evangelize from village to village, nobody wanted to sign up because this hadn't been done before. They were shy, embarrassed, and not bold. Daniel Zu, who was the head of the mission school then, and my closest spiritual partner, translator, and brother in the Lord, had the same vision for evangelism and discipleship as I did. He appointed some of our students—those who had learned the dramas and songs—and told them that they were going. That ended a lot of the indecision, and once they knew they were going on the evangelism trip, they completely committed to practicing and rehearsing what they had been taught. In December we loaded our young new evangelists into outboard motor-powered canoe type boats and went downriver. The Lord really went before us, and with us. We prayed before we left, along the way, and at each village. Many came.

We were able to get *The Jesus Film* from Campus Crusade for Christ in both the Karen and Burmese languages. We had huge reels of film in both 8 mm and 16 mm, ready for wherever the Lord would take us. That meant we had to carry not only the huge film reels, but also transport a very large, heavy generator and fuel up and down jungle mountains. The film ran three to four hours and most people would stay and watch it until the end. Many people came to know Jesus, to understand who He is. Even the Christians that were Christian in name only and just going to church understood who Jesus really is and His love for them. It was exciting to go from village to village. It was always my hope and intention to go back to follow up and see how many people had stayed with the Lord. I was blessed to be able to do this in some villages, but not all.

Many parents moved to Ah Moe village to send their children to Ah Moe Mission School and the community grew from only ten homes to over one hundred. We did not charge any tuition fees if they didn't have any money. Many Buddhist and animist families moved to Ah Moe village to send their children to the school, and many children accepted the Lord. This had an impact on their families as well. The children would explain the Gospel to them when they went back home, becoming little evangelists. During this period two girls from Campus Crusade for Christ in Bangkok came to teach evangelism training. They took the students out into the village, from house to house, and people accepted the Lord. They taught them about "quiet time," and being away to spend time with the Lord. It really strengthened the students. Some families didn't want their children to be baptized because they didn't really understand what it was all about, but the school staff, and sometimes myself, would go with them and explain to the parents the love Jesus has for them and share the Gospel with them. Those families came to the Lord. There were many spiritual battles in them coming to the Lord, but God was faithful, and brought many to Himself.

I was also teaching the Navigator Colossians 2:7 Discipleship Bible study and other Navigator Bible studies at this time. It took years, but eventually the 2:7 Bible study was finally translated into the Karen language. We would have one day of prayer, often on a Saturday, and go out into the jungle to spend time alone with God, then come back together and share what the Lord had taught us through His Word and other books they had read. These were wonderful times of spiritual growth.

Later in 1994, a faith-filled family from Australia came to live in the village for about a year. Jason, Anne, and their seven-year-old son were a blessing to the ministry, and it was great to have some more English-speaking people for me to converse with. They believed God wanted them to be there, but Jason, being the leader of his family, was very fearful because of the war situation and the possibility of the Burmese soldiers arriving. His concerns were not unwarranted. In fact, they were pretty realistic as we would soon find out. He struggled with concern for his family, but God used them all mightily while they were there.

Like me, they had to leave the country every three months to renew their visas. On one of those trips in 1995 his fears were realized; the Burmese came. It was best for all of them, especially their young son, that they had already left the country to renew their visas and didn't have to flee from the Burmese Army. God was in control and protecting them. When they came back from renewing their visas, we had all fled to Thailand. The Thai gave us refuge in a Buddhist monastery for a week. I was able to arrange for most of their family belongings to be sent to the hotel in Kanchanaburi where I knew they would be staying when they came back. After one week, the Thai told us that we had to go back into the jungle. It was not safe to go back to our villages yet because we didn't know where the Burmese were, so when we went back, we had to find new areas to stay that had a source of water. The Australian family decided to go back to Australia, which I understood.

There were three villages that fled during this period, and we had to separate into three different areas so there would be enough water for everybody. The Lord showed us those places and we stayed there for three months until school started again and we could go back to Ah Moe safely. The following two years were exciting and productive. We had three different headmasters at Ah Moe Mission School from 1991 to 1997. The first year it was Thra Htoo Ler and his family, who helped us build the mission school. He was wonderful at organizing everything and through his hard work we got the school built fast. But his first year was a hard one. He was a strong leader, and some Karen were not used to that. They are used to just being appointed and then doing what they were told to do without detailed supervision. So, it was a year of struggle, learning to obey a leader who was strong and persevering, and keeping our eyes on Jesus. We got through that year successfully, and managed to keep all the students and teachers who wanted to leave during that difficult time. Through sharing God's Word with them, especially 2 Peter 2:18, "be submissive to your masters with all fear, not only to the good and gentle, but also to the harsh," and praying, everybody was able to remain strong enough to stay by keeping their eyes focused on Jesus and persevering in Him. It was a wonderful victory for everybody.

The next year, my closest spiritual partner, Daniel Zu, became the principal of the mission school for us. Karen culture is very different from American culture, especially concerning family roles. He said that in order for people to accept him and respect him he would need to get married first. He already had a girlfriend, Beh Beh, who was in my very first discipleship class in 1986 and they had been planning on getting married for a long time. They didn't have funds to get married and live as a family, so I helped them and they wed in Htee Hta village. They stayed in my house there for a while, then when the school opened, they moved to Ah Moe village where he served as headmaster of Ah Moe Mission School. That's when the jealousy started. He was a wonderful headmaster but because he was young, some older Christians thought that they should be in control. They began to make things difficult for him, taking advantage of his youth and inexperience. He wanted to quit many times. But he was committed to the Lord and strong in the Lord, and through much encouragement and prayer, he was headmaster at Ah Moe Mission School for four years. He did a great job, and I really thank the Lord for him.

We had both blessings and trials in abundance at the Ah Moe Mission School during this period. One of the continuing trials was the Australian who came in opposition and continued to sow discord among the villagers, but by now it was harder for him to get people to believe his lies. The villagers had seen, and continued to see, God work and were enjoying the blessings of all we were doing together through Him. I wonder what we could have accomplished if he had come to work with us instead of against us. God doesn't give each of us the same gifts and talents. We are to work together like a family, combining the special resources He has given us to build His Kingdom. Unfortunately, that was not the goal of the Australian.

People began to be a bit suspicious of the Australian then and would ask me questions about him. I'd only heard rumors about him, and I didn't want to spread them because I don't like passing on anything that I'm not sure is true. I was pressed for information by my favorite Karen pastor, Pastor Moses, so, somewhat uncomfortably, I told him what I'd heard, but emphasized that I didn't know if it was true. Circumstances eventually brought the truth to light. Within a few months, the Australian was put in jail for being a pedophile with a young Burmese boy in Australia. Those were the rumors that we had heard, so I guess they were true. I was praying for God's protection for all of the boys in the boy's dorm, that the Australian arranged and provided financially to build. He had stayed with them in the dorm in Htee Hta village while the mission school was being built. He was put on trial in Australia and was convicted. Another good Australian friend said to me, "Never try to touch one of God's anointed people, because it will not succeed." In time, God always judges sin. We cannot live in sin without God's judgement. It may not be swift sometimes, but it comes eventually. At that point, the Thai-Karen who brought him in was too embarrassed to come back, so he did not return to our area any more. God had removed both of those oppositions.

Sharon at eighteen

Sharon's family: daughter Shelly, Sharon, son Brad, Sharon's mother
Helen, daughter Kelly, sister Merrilee, and her son

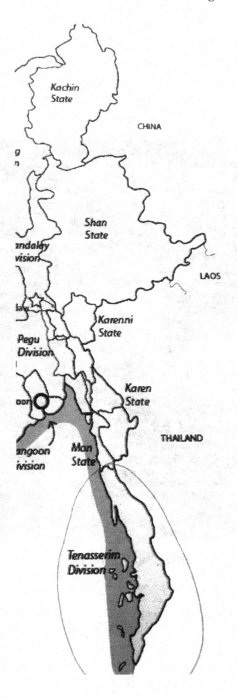

Sharon in Burma 1985

5.   First Class in 1986.

Caring for God's littlest ones

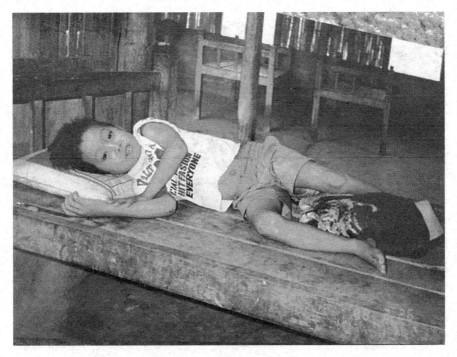

Saw Po Rah in the Htee Hta village hospital

Ler Lah operating the projector on an evangelism trip

Victory! Returning from an evangelism trip

Sharon escaping the Burmese Army through the jungle

Escaping to Thailand

Loading the refugees' belongings on elephants

Sharon crossing border in disguise

Sharon with Cholora

David Eubank

Refugee camp in 1997

Sharon's new car

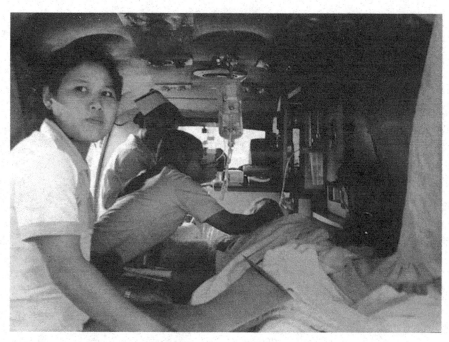

An unexpected ambulance ride

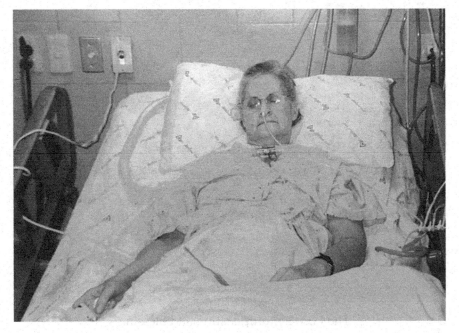

Two months in intensive care

The Lord's multiplication and blessing!

CHAPTER SIX

GOD'S PEACE IN SICKNESS AND WAR

I will lift up my eyes to the hills—
from whence comes my help?
My help comes from the Lord, who made heaven and earth.
Psalm 121:1, 2

A s you can probably tell, by this point in my life I'd
gotten about as far away as one can get from being the
suburban Southern California housewife I thought I
wanted to be. The comforts of my youth were a world away
and I had acquired several new families, in addition to the one
I'd started out with. Besides my own birth children, the Lord
gave me several Karen children who lived with me or were
entrusted into my care as a teacher. I had my family of pastors
and teachers in the jungle villages, and I had a church family
back in the States that provided prayer, love, encouragement,
and enough financial resources to allow me to serve the Lord
on the mission field. There was one family member, however,
who was especially concerned about me. My mother.

Mothers are supposed to be concerned about their children.
That's their job, like it or not. It starts the moment they give
birth and it never ends, no matter how old and independent

that child may be. I was a middle-aged woman who had conquered challenges most people wouldn't even dream of, but my perseverance (and God's obvious protection) didn't do much to calm my mother's fears. I was still her child, no matter what. Being in a primitive location on the other side of the world was bad enough, but when we fled for our lives in 1995 my mother was understandably worried. I always found peace in my faith in God no matter what chaos swirled around me, but my mother didn't have that peace. My mother was not a believer.

Christians can be kind of a mystery to people who have never known a saving faith in Jesus. Some think we're foolish or superstitious, or it's a fad or a phase, and others don't think about us much at all and just regard us as a curiosity. They don't understand the change that comes over our lives when we are born again. For some, an event in life will suddenly cause them to reevaluate faith, and that can be the breakthrough to salvation. The Burmese Army, a half a world away, turned out to be the breakthrough for my mother. The Lord used my fleeing them as a vessel to bring my mother and me into a closer relationship. As it says in the Bible in Romans 8:28, "And we know that all things work together for good to those who love God, and are called according to his purposes." That is one of my life verses, and I thank God for Him using that opportunity to bring my mother close to Him. Within a couple of years, she accepted the Lord, then the Lord called her home about one year later. I really praise God and thank Him for His faithfulness and for answering my prayers for my mother. I prayed for her for twenty-five years. *Never* give up praying. God is faithful. Even if it's not as fast as we want it to be.

Evangelism had been a strange concept to the Karen before then, but by December 1992, so many students wanted to sign up to go and share the Gospel that we didn't have enough boats to transport them. The first year we went in one boat; the second year we had to find two extra boats; then each year after that the number of those who wanted to go and share the Gospel increased. What a wonderful problem to have. In the end, so many were enthusiastic about evangelizing. Like everything else in the area, boats were hard to come by, but the Lord provided three or four at various times and we put our group together. We broke up into three different teams and went in separate directions. One team went upriver to the north, one went to the west to the frontline villages, and one went to the south—way down south as far as we could go. Each team shared the Gospel in villages all along the way. We tried to cover as many villages as possible and we usually traveled for about three weeks. Once it was for an entire month.

God really blessed these trips. I was able to take great videos of our outboard motor canoes going through the rapids, but there was often an added element of excitement. Many times, we would have to get out of the boats and walk on the riverbank, as they could only go through the rapids with the driver and supplies. The river was treacherous and it was very difficult to control the overloaded boats in the turbulent water. More than once they capsized—which was a little more excitement than any of us needed—and we had to go gather our things out of the river. Sometimes the supplies that had fallen overboard rushed downriver, so we'd have to get back in the boat at a safe point and scan the riverbanks as we moved downriver searching for any of our gear that may have washed up on shore. Nature is a beautiful thing, but it can also be very challenging.

The years of 1996 and 1997 were very fruitful, but for some

reason that I didn't understand, the Lord began speaking to me about moving from Ah Moe village. I had two boys living with me at that time. Up until then I had about ten children living with me. They all came to me when they were about twelve years old and went to school from the fifth grade until they graduated from high school. By this time, I had already sent one, Juty, on to the English Bible School course up in Beh Klaw refugee camp. They were all growing up. Moonlight had graduated from high school, studied medicine, and was serving in villages on the frontline of the war zone as well as putting in some time helping us at the school. La Lay Sha had graduated from high school and was studying lab work in Htee Hta village. I asked the two boys living with me, Heh Ney Htoo and Saw Po Rah (because the Lord had put it on my heart that we were not going to be there next year), if they would want to finish their high school education at Beh Klaw refugee camp. They both said they would love to go. Everything seemed to be going well.

In 1997, Reverend Tha Gay became our Ah Moe Mission School headmaster. He remained so from June 1996 until January 1997, when the Burmese Army came the second time. He was a wonderful blessing from the moment he joined us, but he served less than a year before we had to flee. Earlier, when I came back from America in 1996, he asked why I couldn't speak Karen yet. It was a valid and understandable question. I'd been with them for eleven years and really could not yet share the Gospel in the Karen language. It wasn't for lack of trying; I'm just not a linguist. I struggled for hours, days, and years—one year in particular from morning until night. I just don't get languages easily, particularly one that has virtually no similarities to English. Another problem, I told him, was trying to teach English and learn Karen at the same time. I said,

"If you will please tell me that I'm not going to teach English this year, but am going to teach the discipleship course only in Karen, without speaking English, I believe that I will be able to share the Gospel soon." He agreed to that. "No teaching English this year, only speak Karen." That was my first year to teach the discipleship course alone in the Karen language. I already had the discipleship course translated into the Karen language while I was in Htee Hta village. I could read it all right, but could not speak it because I'd always had an interpreter or I'd asked a Karen to teach it for me. This was a big step for me and it paid off. Three months later was December when we were going to go out for our Christmas evangelism trip. As I went with the team, I realized that I could actually finally share the Gospel. I don't seem to be able to do two things at one time, but by just concentrating on the Karen language and using it every day, in three months' time I was able to share the Gospel with the Karen in their own language. Reverend Tha Gay's help in this matter was a major contribution to sharing the Word with the Karen, which helps me to this day.

The jungles of Burma and Thailand are beautiful, but they also seem to have more than their share of natural challenges. The monsoon season brings torrential, relentless rains that pour down more water than the earth can possibly absorb. Rivers and mosquitos rage, and at this particular time, in 1996, we had a landslide. Monsoon-related calamities were to be expected. In fact, every year when I would go back to the States, I would discover something major had happened while I was gone. And nature wasn't the only culprit. Every time I would come back, I found the Lord had changed the ministry from what it was to something new. When I finally realized this was a pattern, which took several years, I would wonder each time I came back what new surprise the Lord had in store for me.

Some people were frustrated with me because when I returned, I didn't know exactly what I was going to do. That was true. I didn't know because the Lord always changed things and I didn't know what to expect until I got there. I would see what He had done while I was gone, and then He would lead me in the direction He wanted me to go. That was a different kind of adventure, but it's really exciting to live for the Lord one step at a time. I cannot even say one day at a time because He'll change things during the day.

Another one of my life verses is Proverbs 16:9 which says, "A man plans his way, but the Lord directs his steps." I have learned through my many years of ministry here that I can plan anything I want, and as soon as I think I have figured out what the Lord wants me to do, He changes it. It's always better, much more exciting, and much more fruitful than what I thought was His plan. There is excitement in seeing God work, so, I am always ready for Him to change anything. It's exciting to be in tune with Him and go along with what He wants to do.

On this occasion, seeing the Lord's new plan had to wait while I figured out how to deal with the landslide. It wasn't just a local problem; it was a personal problem. Our house, which had been on the riverbank, was now hanging on a cliff. I have enormous faith in the Lord's protection, but He also gave me the common sense to figure out on my own that hanging on the side of a cliff was not a great idea. I was going to need a little help, and God promptly sent it.

On one of his early trips, the Australian missionary who kept interfering brought Max Harris, another Australian, with him. Max worked in the Outback area of Australia, digging wells and providing construction help for the sparse population there. He decided he wanted to help the Karen, and joined the Australian missionary. When I first met him, he was running water pipes from the river into village homes. He was installing a pipe into the hut of the woman who lived across from me and wanted to run pipe into my house, too, but the Australian missionary told him not to do it, because I was useless and provided no benefit to the Karen. Fortunately, Max asked the villagers about me and got the truth. From that point on, Max worked with me instead of against me. He made his subsequent visits alone, or with his wife, and was a tremendous blessing to the Karen.

When Max arrived from Australia on this trip, the rain and landslides had changed the terrain dramatically. Max had come specifically to help at the school, but it was immediately obvious to him that my house was no longer safe to live in and needed to be moved. It made me sad because we really loved that home. The Lord had given us the home, built of wood and bamboo, right at the edge of the river, so it was hard for us to see it moved, but it was torn down and reassembled in another location. I guess the fact of the matter was, if we didn't move it, nature eventually would. Max went back to Australia after the house was rebuilt in its new location. He hadn't had time to build a proper toilet, so he returned with his wife, Coralie, in January 1997. Max is a great example of how God uses many people with many skills to do his work. His specialty is to come to these villages and dig wells and build toilets. These are things we take for granted in the States, but they are frequently lacking in the jungle. To have someone come from a country far away and provide these things for the villagers is a great example of Christian love. We are examples by our actions, not just our words.

My years of ministry have been filled with God's blessings and some outright miracles. Heh Ney Htoo falls into both categories. He came to live with me when he was eleven years old, and at the age of sixteen he required surgery. Before Heh

Ney Htoo came to live with me, his younger brother had a large hernia on the outside of his body. After Heh Ney Htoo knew he would be living with me, he prayed and asked the Lord to transfer his brother's hernia over to him, because he knew I would be able to help him and his brother had no way to get any help. Believe it or not, the Lord did transfer the hernia to Heh Ney Htoo. It is still amazing to me that he was willing to take on his brother's suffering. This is supernatural to me, ministers to me, and humbles me so much.

Before I could really understand the Karen language, Heh Ney Htoo told me about his prayer, but I didn't understand what he said. Then, in God's perfect timing, I noticed something was wrong when he returned from bathing in the river. When I asked him about it, he told me the story again. At this same time, I "just happened" to hear that a group of surgeons would be arriving from overseas to Htee Hta village. When I went down river to talk to them, they said they could help him. They operated on this massive hernia and it was very painful, but he was healed. We praise the Lord for the people He sends at just the right time, and thank them for their willingness and obedience to come to the jungle, where He has called them to come.

Heh Ney Htoo's surgery was only about three weeks before the Burmese soldiers came in 1997. He had it in his heart that he wanted to fight; however, when he was born his mother dedicated him to the Lord, to serve the Lord with his life. I also didn't want him to fight. The Lord was faithful to show him how it must not be His will for him to fight, because of his mom's desire, my desire, and the timing of his surgery. I believe there are Christians on the Burmese side and I don't believe the Lord would want a Christian to kill a Christian. He has grown in understanding, though it has been a struggle and has taken years, but God has protected him and chosen him to live for Him and serve Him with his life. I praise the Lord for how He has worked in Heh Ney Htoo's life to bring him to the place He wants him to be. He is now living for the Lord full-time.

In addition to monsoons, landslides, and disease, the mid-90s brought another problem: the war escalated. Control of the area had been in dispute for decades, but I didn't know that situation when He called me. I just obeyed Him. Nevertheless, the Burmese attacked twice during this period and it wasn't the kind of thing I could ignore. My children were in danger, and likely so was I. We had no choice but to pick up what we could carry and leave.

At the beginning of the first attack, when we all had to flee in 1995, Ler Lah, who wanted to protect me, took me out by truck ahead of everyone else. That was something that was extremely hard for me to do. There were no telephones in the village, of course. We heard that the Burmese Army was coming from a man who was passing the village in a boat on the river. He yelled to us that they were twenty minutes away and we had to run immediately to save our lives. That was quite a shock, but strangely, I had a total peace in my heart. It was amazing. I was so calm. I looked at the kids, and said, "Okay, what are we going to do? What are we going to take with us? Let's pack a few things, and let's go." I was calm and particularly pragmatic. What came to my mind to take was my Bible, a roll of toilet paper, my toothbrush, and toothpaste. That's all I put together. The kids stayed calm, too. Then Ler Lah came and told me to leave with him in the mission truck. I initially declined, telling him I couldn't leave my children, but he was adamant. I had to leave right then. We had quite an argument back and forth until he made me realize I was wasting valuable time. Other lives were going to be in danger if I didn't listen to him and obey him, because he wasn't going to help them until he finished helping me. So, he put me in his truck and took me out over the bumpy road. He wanted to take me to another village that he thought would be safe. That started another argument. I told him—most emphatically—that I would only go where I knew I would see my children again. He could tell that he had reached my limit, so he agreed to leave me there to walk out with the other refugees. There wasn't time to create or explain a plan. He just pointed out a direction and told me to keep walking.

I fell in with the sad group of refugees, carrying what was left of their lives on their backs, and we started our trek toward the safety of Thailand. At that moment of discouragement, the Lord gave me a verse that I had never in my life memorized. It totally came to my mind so clear, "I will lift up my eyes to the mountains, from where shall my help come? My help comes from the Lord, who made heaven and earth" (Psalm 121:1 and 2). I was looking at the beautiful mountains of Kaw Thoo Lei, where the Karen lived, and thanking God for giving me this verse, and for showing me that He is my help, and everything will be fine. I walked among the group, many weeping, and I vividly remember one particular woman. She was in tears, and the Lord put it on my heart to ask her if her husband was with her. "Yes," she said. "Are your children with you?" "Yes," she responded again. "Then don't worry about anything else because all that's really valuable is with you, and you will be fine." She was encouraged by that, and we walked on together.

When I got to the border gate crossing into Thailand, I wanted to stay nearby where I would immediately see my children, who I hoped were following close behind. It was bedlam, of course, and a few people were valiantly trying to help direct the mass exodus. Against my wishes, I was guided on to another area. Ler Lah had returned with a whole group of people by then, and organized us to get to a safe place. The villagers in Thailand heard of our plight and immediately got together and started cooking. Hundreds of people came out to help us at that time. The Thai arranged for us to have safe refuge, but my heart was saying, *Where are my children?* I would walk through the village and get as close to the border gate as I could, scanning the area for familiar faces. Eventually, all but two staggered into the place where we were. I worried about the missing ones, of course, but they showed up the next day. They were late because they helped Daniel Zu and his wife, Beh Beh, who already had two children, and was pregnant with her third. They carried their belongings, reassured the children, and did everything they possibly could to help the family escape in time. Everything was made worse because it rained that night and they had to sleep in the downpour with nothing for protection. It's hard to describe what the Karen have gone through, but God did get them all out safely.

The Lord got us all across the Thai borders safely, which was a relief to everyone and prompted lots of thanking the Lord. Our special story of God's presence and protection was told by Max, the well-digger from Australia, who helped us in many ways. He had gone to town to buy supplies, and when he returned, we had all fled to Thailand. He asked the Thai guards where the foreigner was. They said there were three foreigners, but that was impossible because I was the only one. They insisted they saw three. Max's conclusion was the other two were my angels fleeing with me keeping me safe.

Obviously, the situation had been extremely emotional for me and it prompted me to make a decision. I told Ler Lah and everyone else, "Please, do not send me out ahead again." I honestly believe that if God has called me to a people, that He wants me to stay with the people, and go through whatever they go through, even if it brings us all to our end. I am committed to what the Lord has called me to do, and where He has called me to be, until He calls me otherwise. I cannot see fleeing from a ministry that He has called me to so that I will be safe, and they will not. I do not understand that, and I thank the Lord for the conviction that He has given me, and the faith and perseverance He has given me to carry out His will. Each time there has been danger I have had absolutely no fear at all.

Each time there was danger announced, I always had peace. I knew that I was where the Lord wanted me to be. I believed, I was obedient, and I stayed. Others may have different ideas and haven't always understood my faith, but that is how I believe the Lord has called me. It's kind of strange—funny actually. I'm afraid of needle injections, but I was never afraid of the Burmese.

We all survived the 1995 attack, by God's grace. The Thai village leaders arranged for us to stay in an empty school for the first couple of nights, then moved us to stay in a Buddhist temple. They trucked in water for us, and helped us with many things, until they ordered us all to get in their trucks to be taken back over the border to where we fled from. We couldn't go back to the school yet, because we didn't know if it was safe, and two other villages fled at the same time. So, we divided into three groups to "settle" where there were water wells and survived as best we could. That was a very difficult time, but I learned many things on how to survive in the jungle, and still had the Lord's peace. Three months later, after the Karen leaders checked out the situation, we resettled back in our villages and tried picking up where we left off, but the Burmese Army wasn't through with us. They returned in 1997, and again we had to flee. By now we all had a pretty good idea of what we were in for, but the Lord chose this time to give me another verse. As I prayed about what He wanted me to do, He showed me not to go out the way we went out the first time.

When Ler Lah, Daniel Zu, and Reverend Tha Gay came to me and said, "What will you do? Where will you go?" I said, "I don't know. All I know is that the Lord does not want me to go out the same way we went out last time." By this time my trust in the Lord had become contagious, so they trusted me. They told me that they had a plan and I should follow them, so I agreed. As the Bible says, we were "all in one accord." They even wired to the governor of our area to tell him what I said and he said, "It's okay. If that's what she believes she should do, then go ahead and take her with you." We packed up boats and were taken downriver. The whole experience was mildly organized chaos. Everybody was not together all the time, but I had my children, so I didn't have to worry about them like I did two years earlier. For a few, like Daniel Zu and Reverend Tha Gay, we had to wait. Others would follow later. Since we didn't have a lot of boats, the boatman would take us a certain distance down the river, drop us off, and then go back to pick up another group. Once we were all in the same location, the process would start over again with the boats taking us out step-by-step, taking out one group, dropping them off, and going to get the next group. It's certainly not the most efficient way to travel, but it worked. More importantly, we didn't have another option. This whole step-by-step process went on for about a week. I had a video camera at this time and I documented our entire trip. As odd as it may seem under the circumstances, it was so much fun to be like a reporter and record everything that was going on.

We finally put enough distance between us and the Burmese Army, which was a blessing from the Lord, because Reverend Tha Gay was sick with malaria. We prayed for him, built a shelter for our things (it was raining), and cared for him, then all started out walking together toward the Thai border a few days later when he was stronger. It took two or three days, but that was just the beginning of a long, confusing search for safety. We would stop, find shelter along the way, and listen to the news on a portable shortwave radio. No one really knew what to do with us and our whole flight turned into something that resembled a ping-pong match. We would arrive somewhere and the authorities would say we would have to go back to the place we came from and stay there. Later, those authorities would say we could go forward, closer to the border. When we arrived at the new location the new authorities would send us back again. This went on and on for about six weeks. It was exhausting, but we had no choice in the matter, and I was trusting the Lord for His protection. We were traveling by foot and could only carry the barest minimum of personal possessions, but our belongings that had come downriver on the boats with us eventually caught up with us. The Karen leaders arranged for our gear to be loaded on elephants that carried it through the jungle to us at the border.

During this entire six weeks I had the Lord's peace. It's hard to describe. One time I went ahead with four children, and I remembered the movie *Inn of the Sixth Happiness*, when a missionary, Gladys Aylward, was fleeing with one hundred children through China, and arrived safely. I remembered a song from the movie and sang it as I led children through this narrow path where only an elephant had trodden before. On our right was a cliff with a deadly drop-off. I sang that song, remembered how the Lord helped her, prayed, and we got through safely. I thank the Lord so much for His protection and for His faithfulness.

After fleeing for five weeks, we were able to camp along

the borderline for about one week. At this time there were no bathrooms, and the only food we had was what we could scavenge in the jungle. Our particular group of about three hundred people stayed together and many of the Ah Moe Mission School students stayed with us. It wasn't safe to go back to their villages, which were along the Burmese border, so they had to flee with us. To make a bad situation worse, all of them were separated from their parents. It was really hard to watch them not be able to go back home, but the Lord strengthened them, and they helped by looking for vegetables every day. The Lord provided abundantly. We had a little river nearby and there were fish, prawns, and even pollywogs that we ate. (If pollywogs don't sound appetizing, you've probably never been really, really hungry.) We weren't the only ones who got hungry. We had four elephants with us often and they had to find their food in the jungle, too. If they didn't eat—and elephants eat a lot—they wouldn't have the strength to continue to carry all of our stuff for us. Surprisingly, I was probably healthier during that time than any other time I stayed with the Karen. It was all by God's grace. We all had enough food to eat, by God's miraculous provision, from foraging in the jungle, and so did our enormous, four-legged helpers.

After about a week there I wanted to evangelize a group of Pwo Karen Buddhists. As if my struggle to learn to speak Karen hadn't been torturous enough, there is more than one Karen dialect. I had studied Skgaw Karen, not Pwo Karen, so I took one of my children, Moonlight, who is a Pwo Karen, to interpret for me. We were going from shelter to shelter, praying for the sick, and sharing the Gospel from God's Word. They had set up an area with their Buddhist posters and altars, but they welcomed us. I was really excited about this opportunity, but it didn't last long. While we were there, Ler Lah arrived with that unfortunately familiar, urgent expression on his face that said, "Go back to the main road. We need to leave."

When everyone fled from Ah Moe village, Ler Lah went out on the same road on which we fled in 1995. He hired some Thai policemen to get the mission school truck to the area where he knew we had planned to come out. He was able, by God's grace, and the local Thai authorities, to truck in rice to us while we were waiting for permission to cross the border into Thailand for safety. This particular day they said he could not do that because the Thai were instructed to deliver rice to the Burmese soldiers. He informed me of that in the morning and told me not to tell anybody, but just to pray. So I prayed and went on my way to share the Gospel with the Pwo Karen. About three or four hours later he came back and urgently told us to get back to the main road, that we had permission to go out. He told me that when the Thai went to deliver rice to the Burmese soldiers, they realized that they were only one hour by foot away from us. They had almost caught up to us. The Thai would not allow us to come into Thailand until our lives were actually in danger. When they saw that the enemy soldiers were only one hour away by foot, it was clear to them that our lives were at imminent risk. They said, "Okay, you can come into Thailand now." We all packed what we had and walked very quietly to the border.

I cannot remember how many hours it took us to get there. That's probably a good indicator of our physical and mental condition. Time no longer seemed to exist. We climbed a mountain, crossed the border, and had no idea how much farther we had to go. We just kept walking, escorted by Thai soldiers. All of a sudden it started to rain and the soldiers told us we had to stop for the night. We didn't have any tools, so we had to use whatever we could find to clear an area to lie down on the ground and sleep with whatever we had to cover us. The rain continued all night. At daybreak, they came and told us to start walking again. Wet, physically and emotionally exhausted, we marched on. At noon, they let us stop to cook, eat, and take a bath in a big stream that had a few waterfalls we used as showers. Everything looked normal—cooking, bathing, washing clothes, and swimming in the river—but it wasn't. We had no idea where we were, or where we were going. After about two hours they prodded us on again, and again, we had no idea where we were going or how long it would take to get there. We struggled along until I looked up and saw a TV antenna silhouetted against the sky. I smiled and thought, *We won't be walking much farther.* We were walking in an area that was totally uninhabited, yet when I saw the TV antenna, I knew that we must be close to some "civilization." Sure enough, a while later they herded us all into a barren rice field. I say herded because it reminded me of movies, I've seen about people being sent into a concentration camp. That wasn't a very pleasant comparison, but I felt like those poor Jewish people in the films I'd seen. They were numbering us as we went in, counting off one, two, three, four, and so on. I don't remember which number I was. There was nothing there. Absolutely nothing. We were in a barren, dry land withering under the oppressive heat.

After the Thai authorities counted us, the Karen organized who would go out and cut down bamboo, and who could do the other things necessary to set up some sort of rudimentary camping ground. They set up a makeshift clinic, so Moonlight went there to work. Heh Ney Htoo, who was with me, helped people build their temporary shelters. For some reason the Thai wouldn't allow us to elevate the shelters off the ground. That meant we had to sleep on the earth, and since it rained every day, people were sleeping in mud, and on wet ground. The Thai provided everyone with a plastic tarp to use as a covering, but the rain came in and the ground was wet. The whole experience was miserable.

My youngest Karen child, Saw Po Rah, left us while we were fleeing by boat down the river. He got off the boat near his village when his mother asked him to come and help her flee. That was completely understandable, and he did the right thing. That left me with two primary helpers, Moonlight and Heh Ney Htoo. Moonlight was busy helping the sick and Heh Ney Htoo and I were helping others. We had one of the Ah Moe Mission School students helping cook and boil water for us. Having sufficient drinking water was a constant problem. The river for our water supply was small, and about a fifteen-minute walk in the broiling sun. We were told not to wash dirty things, like children's and babies' underwear, in the river, since we needed clean water to drink. I saw several people disregard those instructions which, predictably, had unpleasant consequences later.

We finally arrived in Thailand. There were some stragglers; a few pregnant women stopped to give birth along the way, and some of the older people walked very slowly, but the Thai were helping them. Through this entire perilous trek, we did not lose one life.

I don't know exactly how many people there were in this mass of fleeing refugees, but there were Karen from several villages. We converged on this camp together, swelling the population by thousands. We spent Saturday getting organized, making shelters, and helping the sick people. Easter Sunday, Reverend Tha Gay had a sunrise service, then we went from shelter to shelter and shared the Gospel. We had a special noon service glorifying the Lord—thanking Him for His protection. It was wonderful how all the Christians, who had just lost their land and had only the belongings they could carry on their backs, could actually be praising God.

The Buddhist group was in their own part of the camp, doing their chants in the mornings and in the evenings. I had never been this close to Buddhists while they observed their religious rites. Every time they chanted, I was quietly praying. They ended up not staying, but going back into the jungle. The Christians were daily singing Christian songs, praying, and praising God. It was a blessing because God showed us that we could praise Him, even in the midst of difficulties, even in the midst of losing everything.

Some mission organizations heard what had happen to the Karen, so they brought as many things to us as they could to help. The clothes, however, were mostly ragged, torn, and dirty. They weren't fit to be worn by anybody and that made me very sad. All along the way, the Lord was showing me the things I had that I needed to share with others who didn't have anything. Some people fled with only the clothes they had on, so I gave out what I had as I saw the needs. I had very little to begin with and, eventually, I got down to two sarongs. I needed one for wearing and one for bathing. The scripture says, if you have two, you're to share one with those who don't have anything. I had heard about an elderly lady who had only one torn sarong to wear. Ler Lah reminded me of the above scripture, so I gave her my extra sarong, the one I'd used for bathing. From then on, I would bathe in the sarong I was wearing and then walk around in it until it dried. Fortunately, that doesn't take long in Thailand, because it's hot. Anything we had on, even if it was sopping wet, would be totally dry in a few minutes.

During this week, because some were not following the sanitary rules at the river water supply, the inevitable happened and I ended up getting sick. We had a young student boiling our drinking and cooking water, and when I began not feeling well, I started to pay attention to the way she was doing it. She didn't let it boil for ten to fifteen minutes, which is critical with contaminated water. As soon as it boiled, she took it off the fire. I asked her if that was the way she always did it and she said, "Oh yes! I didn't know I was supposed to boil it any longer!" That was the moment when I knew why I had gotten sick. I continued to get sicker and sicker, and there were no toilets, only little, thin bushes to retreat behind for some small degree of privacy. One time, when I had run to the brush, right smack in front of me was this beautiful, little yellow flower. Only one. One lone flower in all the area around me. Yellow is my favorite color. I believe it was the Lord's sign to me, saying, "Everything is going to be okay. You have life, there is life in Me, you will live." The diarrhea got worse to the point where I couldn't even flee to an area that was private. One loses all vanity and becomes very humble in situations like this. It's just what you have to do. Even my son, Heh Ney Htoo, had to go and cover up after me. The Lord, again, continued to give strength. I could see Him in all of it. And I was grateful for Heh Ney Htoo.

Then I got worse. I became so sick that I couldn't even get up anymore. The concern for me by the Karen was touching. People were coming to me and bringing me everything they had, which meant that they had very little left for themselves. I had come to serve them, not be served, and I realized I was beginning to be a burden to them, yet how was I going to get out of this camp? I had fled the jungle, so the Thai officials had authority over me, but this time, beautifully, I was in the country legally. I had official permission from the border when I went into Ah Moe village. I had signed my name and they had my passport number, so they could trace what I was doing in there and how I got in there. It was legal and I came out with everybody else.

This had not been the situation until recently. The Thai authorities closed the border when we fled the first time in 1995. I was now experiencing God's miracle of perfect timing, because for the last two years I had been crossing into Thailand and back, through the jungle and mountains, surreptitiously. I dyed my brown hair black and covered my skin with tanning lotion, which turned a bit yellow, but toned down my telltale white complexion. This worked as long as I kept my distance from any sharp-eyed Thais. These trips were essential. I needed to go back and forth to Thailand to renew my visa, buy supplies, and do all the other tasks associated with living in that environment.

Some of the border crossings were more challenging than others. During this time, on one of my trips to Thailand escorted by my Karen friends, I intended to get out of the truck and walk around the police border check as I usually did. Unfortunately, on the way to the border the truck got stuck in the mud. After a great deal of grunting and groaning, they muscled it out of the mire, but it was then too late for me to get out of the truck and walk down the mountain before dark. Someone came up with a novel solution to the problem: they would hide me in an empty oil drum and pray that they could drive me across the border through the police checkpoint safely. Not exactly first-class travel, but the plan sounded like it could work, so I sat down on the bed of the pickup truck and they placed an empty steel drum over me. Packed up like freight, with my fervent prayers echoing in the drum, they drove down the mountain for thirty or forty minutes to the police border checkpoint. My prayers were answered, and we passed across the border with no questions asked. That was a miracle. After all, how could I reasonably explain being in oil drum? God's Word in Psalm 121:8 came to mind. "The LORD shall preserve your going out and your coming in from this time forth, and even forever more." My barrel ride lasted for another twenty or thirty minutes as I thought, *Now that I'm in here, how are they going to safely get me out without being noticed?* Fortunately, before they had to drive too much farther, they found a secluded spot to pull over and extract me from the barrel unnoticed. Many years have passed since that trip, and it remains a favorite story among the Karen, always bringing laughter. It was definitely a memorable experience for me, too.

Those memories were an encouragement to me as I lay there, terribly sick, not knowing how to get out and get help. The frugal supplies at the clinic they had set up were no help. So again, God, in His faithfulness, sent His angel. This time it was an American missionary in Thailand who I had just met in January, right before we fled. He came in with another person, who I don't even think was a Christian. That person was a journalist. He came into the shelter where I was, and started asking me questions, but I was too weak to talk much. I asked him who he came with and he told me, "David." I said, "Would you please ask David to come see me?" When David came, he asked me what I was doing there. I responded, "The same question goes for you!" He said, "The Lord wanted me to come here and find out how I could help. You don't look very good." I was honest with him and told him I was very sick. He asked if I needed to go to the hospital and I told him that I believed I did. In my heart I knew God had sent me to be a blessing to the Karen, and in my present condition, it would be a blessing to leave them so they didn't have to care for me. David didn't hesitate. "Okay. I will take you out."

As is usually the case in ministry, it was easier said than done.

CHAPTER SEVEN

AN "ANGEL" TO THE RESCUE

For I know the thoughts that I think toward you, says the Lord,
thoughts of peace and not of evil, to give you a future and a hope.
Then you will call upon me and go and pray to me,
and I will listen to you. And you will seek me and find me,
when you search for me with all your heart.

Jeremiah 29:11-13

I don't believe most people want to be deliberately difficult. I believe most people genuinely want to be helpful, but they belong to organizations with rules and governments with laws, and the end result is that they sometimes seem to not be able to get out of their own way. I believe the Thai authorities had sympathy for me, since they could clearly see I was very ill, but they were tangled up in government red tape and it was going to require someone with a very authoritarian presence to cut through it. Fortunately for me, that person was my rescuing "angel" David Eubank and he is not the kind of man who takes no for an answer.

David grew up in a missionary family and had lived in Thailand off and on since he was about six months old. He went to the United States to get an education and then joined the US Army where he became a Ranger and then an officer in the Special Forces, but God called him back to the mission field. Today he has a dynamic ministry called the Free Burma Rangers and has dedicated his life to saving lives and souls along the Thai-Burma border, frequently putting his life on the line to save others. To make his story even more amazing, his wife and three children have gone with him since their children were newborns. If ever a family was under the protective hand of God, it's the David Eubank family. As a person who fearlessly and frequently subjects himself to gunfire for the Kingdom of God, David wasn't about to be delayed by a couple of well-meaning, but slightly befuddled, government officials.

The Thai authorities were concerned that my leaving the camp presented an immigration problem. I was in no condition to present my case, so I found a little piece of shade from the blazing sun and squatted, suffering quietly in silence, while David took charge. The Thai officials spent about a half-hour calling higher authorities without a successful solution, and then David had enough. He threw the weight of his well-known ministry organization into the problem and gave them the solution they had not been able to find on their own. Speaking in fluent Thai he said, "Okay, if it's an immigration problem they'll get her at the airport when it's time for her to leave. Don't worry about it, it's not your responsibility." That worked. The Thai officials would get off the hook by making me someone else's problem.

David loaded me into his truck and we got moving, but I was miserable. He had to stop several times along the way so I could run off into the brush and deal with my persistent physical problem. We finally got to Kanchanaburi where he got me safely on a bus to Bangkok. That part of the trip was only slightly better, in that I didn't have to run off into the bushes every time nature called. Instead, I had to struggle to move my feverish, aching body down the aisle to the tiny bus bathroom four different times as we weaved around corners and jolted over the numerous potholes in the road. The trip took two hours, but it seemed much, much longer.

After arriving in Kanchanaburi I called another missionary friend, Paul, in Bangkok and asked him to meet me, knowing that I was going to need help. He readily agreed, but like everything else on the trip it didn't go smoothly. When I got to Bangkok, I couldn't find him. He was walking around looking for me, and I was walking around looking for him. Moving was incredibly painful, but after an agonizing hour we finally found each other. His plan was to take me to his house, but he took one look at me and questioned if that was a good idea. Was I contagious? I had absolutely no idea. He had two children, and whatever I had he certainly didn't want passed on to them. He quickly came up with another plan; he would take me to a Christian guesthouse near his home. They would be happy to accommodate a missionary. I wish I could say that was the end of my problems, but my stay at the guesthouse is a story in itself.

The managers of that Christian guesthouse were away on a break. They had left a young, single girl in charge, but she did little more than keep the doors open. My friend Paul's wife, Judy, came over once a day to bring me some food, but this wasn't like staying in their house. They were very busy and she could only stop by briefly, then I was on my own for another day. There was a kitchen and some food in the guesthouse, but I was too sick to prepare anything for myself. Consequently, I only ate once a day. What little I ate didn't stick around; I continuously had diarrhea. Despite having a decent place to rest, the sickness was persistent and I got weaker and weaker. I was also troubled by the knowledge that calling for help wasn't much of an option. The telephones were downstairs and the rooms were upstairs, and I was too weak to use the stairs. The only person I could call without a telephone was God. I just kept praying for wisdom because I knew that if I stayed in that situation I would die.

I knew the Lord had promised to protect me, so I kept praying for wisdom of who to call if I could summon the strength to make it downstairs. I suddenly remembered a very good, faithful friend, Margaret Janzen, who had always helped me when I needed it, especially when I was sick. She lived in Chiang Mai, which is twelve hours away from Bangkok by car, but I knew she would do anything in her power to help me, especially if I were in need. My problem was I didn't have her phone number because she had recently changed it. I didn't know what to do, so for three days I just kept praying for wisdom. The Lord reminded me of a coworker of Margaret's, Mary, who was with the OMF Mission Organization, so I slowly made my way downstairs to the reception desk to ask the receptionist to call OMF. We had no cell phones in those days. She called the OMF guesthouse in Bangkok, who gave her Mary's number, then called Mary, who gave her Margaret's number. She then called Margaret for me. Margaret told me to get on the first airplane, assuring me that she would take care of me. I had her talk to the receptionist at the guesthouse who called the airport, but all the flights were full. She had to call Margaret back, who told her to put me on the waiting list. To make a long story short, with a high fever and feeling like I was already dead, I went back to my room and collapsed on my bed.

Then the Lord miraculously opened the door for me to get on a plane that day. The receptionist came up to my room and said, "You're leaving. You've got a flight. You've got half an hour to get ready." I managed to get myself showered, but I only had the same clothes that I'd been wearing for the last ten days. They called a taxi for me, so I took it from the guesthouse to the airport, got on the airplane, and arrived in Chiang Mai feeling and looking like a dirty rag doll. Margaret took one look at me, put me in her car, took me to her home, and said, "You're not to get up. You are to stay here and rest for two months. I don't want to hear any argument from you." I thought at that point, *Okay, I don't feel well enough to do anything anyway.*

Somehow, the Lord had revealed my situation to her and she was prepared for my arrival. She had new nightgowns and sets of underwear already stocked in a closet for me, ready to replace my well-worn clothes.

The amazing thing was, I couldn't eat. Nothing digested, nothing settled, not even rice. I couldn't even drink my favorite drink, Diet Coke. I could only eat soft boiled things, and very little of that. But slowly, because of the Lord giving Margaret wisdom, she got me stronger and stronger, day by day. She was amazed. In about a week, I started worrying about everybody else who had fled. How could I be in an air-conditioned room, being so well taken care of, while the Karen were fleeing, dying, and giving birth along the way, some still hiding in the jungle, and some in the three refugee camps arranged by the Thai? I did not know where my Karen daughter, La Lay Sha was. She had been learning how to work in Htee Hta's hospital's basic medical lab, so when we were fleeing, we stopped in Htee Hta village along the way and found her at the hospital. She said, "I will not go with you. I will stay here, and take care of these soldiers who are wounded and brought to the hospital." She was committed to her people and I totally respected and admired her for her decision. Furthermore, I believed she was right. At that point my problem was that I had no idea where she was, or even if she was still alive. That was really hard for me. I had heard that Saw Po Rah, my youngest, who was with his mother, had also fled, but I didn't know where he was, either. These circumstances placed a great burden on my heart and I could not rest. I was physically depleted, but I still had enough strength to pray.

At this time, my daughter Shelly, in America, was also going through a hard time. She was looking for a safe place for her and her children to go because she was being threatened by her ex-husband. I was praying for her situation. Even though I was physically unable to do anything, I felt guilty that I had the luxury of an air-conditioned room in which to recuperate, when so many others were suffering through situations in surroundings that were much more primitive and difficult. Margaret helped me get through this by providing a much-needed dose of common sense. Eventually, I was able to phone my daughter and find out that she and her children were safe and staying with my other daughter. But where my Karen children, students, and friends were, I did not know. Their flight from the Burmese Army had scattered them everywhere. There was no plan; they just ran wherever they thought was safer at that moment and many ended up hiding in the jungle of their hard-fought-for homeland. This weighed heavily on me, and Margaret could tell I needed a diversion from my worrying, so she bought some cross-stitching for me to do. Between that and my prayers I did my best to calm my spirit while in my room recovering.

After a month, Max, who had served the Karen so faithfully digging wells and building toilets, called from Australia and asked if there was anything he could do to help me. I was uncertain at first, but then I realized that if he could join me and drive, we would be able to go and look for my Karen children. I was not going to be at peace until I knew they were safe. I was worried about everyone, Daniel Zu, Beh Beh, the school staff, and the villagers we had evangelized and worked with. I just wanted to know where they were, how they were, and their situation. He agreed to come, although I don't remember clearly how or through whom. Through my ministry friends, Paul and Judi, the Lord provided a vehicle for us. Max came and picked me up at Margaret's house. Margaret was still worried about me and wanted me to rest for another month, but I just couldn't stay still without knowing how and where everybody was. There was no way to contact them, no phones, nothing, so it was a situation where they had to be searched out. I was going to be sick regardless, so I thought I could at least try to be productive as I recovered.

The Lord was amazing as always, to enable us to do this. Max drove back down south, and the Lord opened doors that man cannot open. He arranged things that we could not arrange ourselves. For example, there "just happened" to be an MSF humanitarian medical organization worker available who was helping those who fled. MSF was the Non-Government Organization (NGO) that was helping the refugees, and the leader then "just happened" to be an American from Newport Beach, California. He was only there during that time; after I found everybody he went back to America, and he's never come back. He was another angel that the Lord sent to help me, just like He sent David to get me out of the camp when I was sick. I know that the Lord sent him. This was the same situation. He instructed us to follow his truck so the authorities would assume we were with him. That worked. We followed his truck, and went straight into the area. I can't even call it a camp. It was just a refugee area that they put the people in with make-shift shelters. You could even see the Burmese at the top of the hill, overlooking this area that they could shoot down into anytime. It was definitely not safe, but it was the only place the Thai allowed them to go.

This particular area was where La Lay Sha was. I was able to find her and have a reunion with her, all the medical workers she was working with, and everybody else there. There were many people that I knew there. I was able to find out whether they were okay or not. Some were sick and one of our mission school students had been shot in his leg. We were able to go out and get medicine arranged for them. So many different people and so many different situations.

There was a middle area that I don't remember how we got into, but somehow we did. God got us into all three areas, by His grace, so that I could find out where everybody that I knew was, how they were, if they needed anything, and if we could help. We helped in many different ways. Whether it be clothing, blankets, medicine, food—anything. We helped as we could. After Max got me into each place to find out where and how everyone was, he returned to Australia. Then I was able to contact other people, and the Lord got me into each of these individual places, in miraculous ways each time. Eventually they put them all together into one camp, which is now called, Tham Hin Temporary Camp, which made it easier. Ler Lah was still outside, so he was the one who was able to take me into these places, or find people to take me into these places, so that I could visit and help as the Lord wanted me to.

In Tham Hin camp, where everybody ended up staying, I was actually able to go in and stay—to sleep, pray, and help as the Lord led. That was a very, very, special time. Moonlight and Heh Ney Htoo were there. Later, Moonlight's younger brother, Sunday, who had lived with us before, arrived at the camp. Before we fled, he had gone back to his village to help his parents. After we fled, his parents sent him to be with

Moonlight to try to continue his education. Eventually, I sent Heh Ney Htoo, Saw Po Rah, Sunday, and some others up to Beh Klaw refugee camp to finish their education, and go to Bible school after they finished high school there. There were no schools in Tham Hin camp at this point. One of the guards said that they would not bless them in building schools. I remember saying to him, "If you don't build schools, these teenagers are going to be restless, and they're going to be causing trouble that they wouldn't cause if they had a school to go to." He listened to that, and agreed, because teenagers aren't going to sit still. They're going to go out into Thailand illegally, and try to find work to survive, or do whatever they want to do if they don't have something planned for them. So, he helped start arranging schools. They started with primary, however, and I think it took two years before they ever had a high school.

Things have become better through the years in the camp, as far as arranging for education, but health care is still very minimal. They are restricted as to what medications they can use. So I send in other medications that people need and that have been given to them by other doctors, that the NGOs are not able to give to them because of orders from their organization headquarters. For example, one of my former students that I sent to Bible school, Bah Bluit Moo, had a stroke while he was at school. He was twenty-nine years old. I was able to arrange for the NGO in Beh Klaw to send him to the local hospital in Mae Sot. They said he had to be transferred to another hospital in Chiang Mai. After many challenges, he finally received brain surgery, then was rehabilitated at McKean Hospital in Chiang Mai. They tried several medicines for him for his high blood pressure, and only one worked. That one was not offered by this NGO medical group, so it had to be arranged from the outside for him. That is one of the ways that

God was using the support that was sent to me to help these special people that He brought into my life. I was there, I knew their needs, and I understood their circumstances. I thank God for this unique opportunity to help His children who have no other way to get help. It was a wonderful blessing.

As 1997 drew to a close, my health was returning and I was reunited with my children, anxious to see what adventures and challenges the new year would bring.

CHAPTER EIGHT

THE PLIGHT OF THE REFUGEES

And I thank Christ Jesus our Lord who has enabled me,
because He counted me faithful, putting me into the ministry,
although I was formerly a blasphemer, a persecutor,
and an insolent man;
but I obtained mercy because I did it ignorantly in unbelief.
And the grace of our Lord was exceedingly abundant,
with faith and love which are in Christ Jesus.

1 Timothy 1:12-14

T he Bible tells us to walk by faith. As a young woman I wasn't able to understand that, let alone do it, but when I committed my life to the Lord, I found a sense of peace that gave me the confidence to keep moving forward, even when I wasn't sure where I was going. I felt very deeply about sharing the love of Jesus, and discipling the Karen, but as my work among them changed, I could see how the impact of missionary work could extend beyond spiritual salvation and impact the physical life of these people. I couldn't possibly have planned any of this; God simply guided me in His own time.

Moonlight had been tending to the physical needs of the people at Tham Hin camp by working as a nurse, something she really enjoyed. Unfortunately, the NGO that supported her work had many rules about what could and could not be done. As she considered what to do, the Lord put it on her heart to go to Bible school. She would increase her knowledge of the Bible and still be able to use her medical knowledge when the opportunity arose. There were other young people in the camp who also wanted to go to Bible school, so I sent them as a group to the Bible school at Beh Klaw refugee camp. This was a wonderful opportunity for them all.

They had a special Bible course that was taught in English, so they would also be able to learn the English language. The curriculum is taught by Baptist seminary graduates from Nagaland, in northeast India. English is their second language. India is certainly not free from its own problems, but these dedicated young people were excited about carrying God's Good News of the Lord to people even less fortunate. They were special people led by a special man, Reverend Simon. He graduated from seminary in Burma, then he went to the Baptist seminary in the Philippines to continue his education. When he completed his studies he returned to Burma, which was when God gave him a burden to help his people who were living in the war zone.

When God gives you an assignment you know it, but it's not always easy. Maybe He leaves the challenges in to test our faith, strengthen us, and help us to grow in our relationship with Him. I do not know. I came to the mission field alone, which was certainly difficult for me. In the case of Reverend Simon, it was quite different. He was accompanied by his entire family, along with his wife's parents, and her brothers and sisters. He was not only responsible for carrying out the mission that God gave him, but he had the added responsibility of caring for many people who were dear to him. They came through the jungle with Thra Htoo Ler, who was our first Ah Moe Mission School principal. A very unique and gifted family. I was thrilled about this because I knew it was a good situation for my children, and other students who had been at Ah Moe Mission School, who wanted to go to Bible school.

Getting these people to the Bible school was a challenge. (There was certainly nothing new about that.) The first problem was very basic: no one had legal traveling papers. They set out completely by faith, with a 100 percent certainty in their hearts that God was sending them, therefore He would make a way. I had to travel separately from them, and was expecting to see them when I arrived, since they should have been there first. They weren't. Having faith does not mean you never worry, especially about your children. I was confident that God would take care of them, but I'm not good at waiting without having any information. Fortunately, the wait was fairly short. They arrived about four hours later, much to my relief, and God brought every single one of them through the long journey to the refugee camp safely. I praise Him for His faithfulness and for His provision, to answer the hearts' cries and the desires of those whom He has chosen—who want to live for Him and serve Him with their lives.

Living in a refugee camp is a hardship, but at that time the living conditions in Beh Klaw refugee camp were the best of any of them, and God arranged His blessing of a Bible school right in the midst of this vast camp. This is the oldest of the camps, having been there for over forty years at that point, which is a clear indication of how long this war has been going on. Children who were born there were now middle-aged. At the time I sent them to Bible school, there were almost 40,000 people in this camp. In Tham Hin camp, which is the biggest camp in the south, there were about 10,000 people. The other camp in the south is called Ban Dong Yang camp, which housed about 3,500 people, at that time. There is really no such thing as complete safety in the camps. They are along the Thai/Burma border and frequently experience attacks, or the threat of attacks, from the Burmese military, even though they are located in Thailand. We have always been grateful to the Thai for allowing them to be in Thailand. Though they are not entirely safe, it would be much, much worse without their support.

Altogether there were about 150,000 refugees in all nine of the camps along the Thai/Burma border at the time. However, there were people coming across the border every day fleeing for their lives, looking for food, looking for medicine, looking for clothing, coming into these camps in fear and desperation. Some of them go back, some of them stay. The refugee families that were already there willingly shared their rations with them, but it was not an easy situation. There were still about two million people in the jungle fleeing for their lives every day. They are called Internally Displaced People (IDPs). They had to survive day by day with the Burmese hunting them, fleeing when they heard the Burmese soldiers were coming to burn down their villages and rice fields, or take all their rice supply. One of the camps in the north, Kwey Ker Loh, was completely destroyed. After three attacks the refugees fled farther from the border and the Burmese. They were combined with another camp, Umphang, that had also been attacked in another area, so they had to move it, too, raising the population to about 20,000. There is no way to be completely safe, but the refugees do their best to be as safe as possible. Tragically, it just keeps going on and on with no end in sight. This human crisis has existed since 1947.

I'm blessed to be able to say that the education of the children was a complete success. They finished high school and went on to Bible school, graduating, and most of them have gone on to serve their people and the Lord. To be equipped to serve their own people was something I strongly felt was important for the children. I told them before I arranged for them to go to the Bible school at the refugee camp in the north, that the fruit that they learned at the Bible school in Beh Klaw refugee camp, they needed to bring back down to the south, where there was basically no spiritual life and no fruit. They need to come down and carry on the discipleship, evangelism, and the teaching of the Karen people in the south. By God's grace, five of those I sent to the Bible school became staff at the Bible school that the Lord arranged in central Thailand, along the Thai/Burma border. I usually say south, which means the southern Karen State/Tenasserim area on the Burma side, which is Sangklaburi down to Chumphon on the Thailand side. That's very general, but there are thousands of Karen all along the border between these two points. This is the area that the Lord called me to in 1985. There are many needs in the north and many missionaries are helping the Karen there. I was the only missionary in the southern Karen State from 1985 to 2002 with the Karen in the south. The task was daunting, but I never doubted that God would send help. I knew I was working on his timetable, not mine.

My seventeen years of prayers were answered in November 2002, when the Lord provided me with a wonderful coworker. Her name is Shaune, and with her young daughter, Shalise, she came to minister with me to serve the Karen. Shaune had been homeschooling Shalise for two years at that point, and doing a wonderful job of it, but being a mother and a teacher, in addition to helping me, certainly added to her responsibilities. She began to work at the Thai Karen Bible Institute, the school that the Lord provided about three years before, teaching them about

Easter/Resurrection Sunday. The crucifixion and resurrection of Jesus is the foundation of our belief. It is so important for everyone to understand that Jesus paid the price for our sins, and by his suffering and death we are saved. I've always felt that telling this story was one of the primary reasons God sent me to this area.

For those of us who were raised in the United States, Christianity is part of our culture and we grew up with it. Even nonbelievers generally know enough about it to understand the basic concept that Jesus died for our sins. In other parts of the world, explaining that concept, and why we celebrate it, is not always easy. In Burma, they celebrate Jesus' resurrection on Easter Sunday, and in many areas, they celebrate in a very big way, much as we do in the United States. Thousands of people attend Easter services. Even those who don't know the Lord come and they listen to the Gospel. When I spent my first years in Htee Hta village, Easter Sunday came and went. There was nothing. It was so quiet. I thought, *What can I do? I'm not a creative person. I don't even know what to tell them to do.* But when I went to the pastor and tried to explain it, he said, "We don't know what to do. You need to teach us."

The next Easter Sunday, the Lord gave me something to give to them, so we arranged a program and had a sunrise service. Before the sun rose, one of the villagers, (one of my favorite people, Pu Cha), went around the village ringing a bell, saying, "The Lord has risen! The Lord has risen!" Many villagers came to see what it was all about and it was a very special service. But the next year I was back in America. I had asked the pastor to conduct the Easter service while I was gone, but when I came back, he said, "No. We can't do it if you're not here." It has always been very difficult for me to understand things like this, but I've always accepted it as an indication that my work here is not done and God wants me to stay and finish the job. I don't know if I would go so far as to say I was frustrated, but when the pastor would continue to say things like, "We can't do it on our own," I have to admit that I was a bit puzzled. As the years have passed, I've learned that it just takes time, sometimes it takes years to enable people to really understand what you're teaching them.

Discipleship is not a quick thing under any circumstances, but being in a war zone adds a significant complication. People are understandably fearful, particularly of strangers and people from other cultures. When I left my safe, peaceful home in Southern California it never occurred to me that there was a place where people lived moment by moment, never having any real assurance of safety or security. It takes a long time for people in these violent circumstances to really be able to trust you, and to understand that you are really there because you love them. Strangely, that lack of trust became part of my problem learning the Karen language. Being oppressed and persecuted people, many had a very low self-image. It seemed as though they didn't want to teach me their language, because if they did, I would understand who they really are, and I wouldn't love them. This went on for three years, and finally, when the Lord led me to Emilie Ballard, who had written the only language book, they realized that I was serious; that I was going to learn it no matter what. When one of the kindergarten teachers finally agreed to teach me, it was a whole new relationship and situation. Once I learned their language, I could explain to them that we are all sinners, like people are all over the world, but I still loved them. When they realized this, everybody relaxed. It was spiritual. It's hard to explain. Ministry was open then, and it was such a joy. Even in the midst of all the trials that were going on and the opposition from outside, the relationship with them has been one of trust and love. The Lord continues to show me, step by step, what it is He's called me to do. It's not always the same thing, but the foundation for the things in the future took years to establish. Being in a war zone, the Karen don't readily trust anybody, even each other, so the fact that they would trust me at all is by God's grace.

One of the things that also has established that trust was the fact that I fled the Burmese with them. That gets brought up even today, everywhere I go. When they introduce me in any meeting or church, they say, "This is the one who fled with us when we had to flee from the Burmese, who is committed to us, and who is committed to loving Jesus and serving Him among us." The Lord re-confirms it all the time, as they continue to introduce me that way. That was something that blessed the Karen beyond anything I could have imagined or thought. I am so grateful to the Lord for leading me to do that and giving me His faith, peace, strength, and perseverance, because it really was a joy . . . for me it was not a sacrifice. It is such a blessing to see that it was a blessing for them also. I praise His name.

After we fled in January of 1997, and Max had come and taken me to see where everybody was, I continually asked the Lord, "Now that we're not in the jungle anymore, do You still want me here? If You still want me here, what is it You want me to do?" It was just step by step, and day by day. He always continued to faithfully lead me. The Lord has always had plenty for me to do. Faith can be an encourager of the persecuted and oppressed, but the Karen have a multitude of physical needs as well. The Lord opened the way in the camps to arrange and send clothing, medicine, food, vegetables, and protein. They were supplied by the biggest NGO that helps them, with rice, salt, some oil, some yellow beans, and fish paste (fermented fish, which they use for their seasoning). They are supplied a ration of those, but no vegetables, no meat, nothing like that. This is the main thing that the Lord led me to use my support for in both refugee camps in the south. God faithfully provided for those things for 13,500 people, a remarkable work.

As the Lord increased the ministry, He also faithfully increased the support. When I first came in 1985, I never asked for support because I knew that the Lord would provide. After all, He was the one who called me here. I didn't expect him to make my life easy, but I always knew I would receive what the Lord knew I needed and I was totally at peace with that. In the beginning, when the ministry was small and I was just establishing relationships and teaching one discipleship class, my support was fifty dollars a month. That was the exact amount I needed for traveling and renewing my visa every three months. The Lord knows our needs and He will provide for them. As I said before, it has been so exciting to be on this adventure of life with Him, and to be totally dependent on Him to provide whatever the needs are, whoever He wants to help. He has provided for all that He has wanted me to do. I continually praise Him for His faithfulness.

After we fled in 1997, and I found out how and where everybody was, the Lord put handicapped people on my heart. The first one was Bah Bluit Moo, the one I mentioned before, who had a stroke at twenty-nine years old. I "just happened" to have just come back from America, and was visiting my children at Beh Klaw refugee camp, when he had the stroke. I'd only been there less than a day. These are the kinds of things that I see God's timing in, and know that I am where I'm supposed to be, when I am supposed to be there, even though I don't know anything ahead of time. From that experience, I learned about

McKean Rehabilitation Center in northern Thailand. After taking Bah Bluit Moo there, I suddenly realized there were other handicapped Karen I could help. One of them was one of our former Ah Moe Mission School teachers who, when we were fleeing in 1997, stepped on a land mine which blew his leg off from the knee down. As if the damage and emotional trauma from the blast weren't enough, the treatment at the government hospital left much to be desired. His leg simply wasn't healing, so I sent him to a hospital down in the south in Ratchaburi to have a clean amputation. Now that I was aware of the McKean Rehabilitation Center, I saw the opportunity to help him regain his mobility by being fitted there for a prosthetic leg. There was no such treatment available in the south at the time, so McKean was truly a life-changing experience for him. It was also something of a life-changing experience for me, in the sense that it opened up opportunities to serve the many handicapped Karen people I had met in the villages where I had served. One was in Htee Hta village, the first village I lived in. He was a little boy with cerebral palsy. I ended up sending him to McKean with his sister, to help take care of him. I was able to send many handicapped people there from the south.

Two children were sent by another American girl, Anne, who had visited Chumphon refugee camp. She had been able to transport them up to McKean Rehabilitation Hospital also. It was such a joy and a blessing to meet her, and see her love for the Karen people. She went back to the States to go to medical school because she wanted to build a hospital in Thailand that would staff Karen nurses and doctors who will be able to speak to patients in their own language. It's really hard for Karen to come out into the hospitals in Thailand because they don't speak Thai, and the language barrier makes it difficult for the doctors and nurses to take proper care of them.

Meanwhile, caring for the handicapped continued, such as Mu Kwa in Chumphon refugee camp who the Lord showed me out of the corner of my eye, as he was walking some distance away from me on crutches. I felt the Lord leading me to call out to him and I asked him if he would like to have a prosthetic leg. He had never dreamed anything like this was even possible and he was so happy to go to McKean Rehabilitation Center for that life-changing procedure. That is part of my joy working with the handicapped, to know that their lives truly are changed, both physically and spiritually.

Nothing in that war-torn country is ever easy. At one point, when the war escalated, the Thai director of McKean Hospital told me that all of the patients had to go back because none of them had legal papers. I understood. At that point there were still three patients left who were all from different camps. One was Moonlight's cousin from Beh Klaw refugee camp. She has a debilitating progressive muscular disease. One was from Tham Hin camp, who was all rolled up in a ball before we took him. It was some neurological disease I cannot even name. They did several different surgeries on him and now he can sit up, move his hands a bit, and function in a sitting position, rather than just laying down in a ball. I love the big smile he greets me with when I visit him. It's such a blessing to see that in someone who couldn't do anything before. The third child has polio and had to be returned all the way back down to Chumphon camp, so I had to make three different trips to three different camps. I praise the Lord they all got back safely. Handicapped people remain on my heart and I continued to do my best, with God's help, to make their lives better.

Eventually an NGO was organized, called Handicap International (HI). They have gone into Beh Klaw refugee camp and taught the Karen how to make prostheses, but help does not readily come to the camps in the south. HI only comes once every six months, so I continue to try to help them as I can by providing food, medicine, or whatever is needed for them.

I am so grateful to McKean for all of the help they have provided for these children, and for these handicapped people. I pray that the Lord would provide even more workers to come and fill the gap that is here in the south. The needs continue as new handicapped children are born, and others need recurring care as they grow and need bigger crutches and braces. We do our best, but it frequently seems overwhelming. I am not able to do everything that the Lord puts on my heart. I continually have to pray for His priorities, do only the things that He wants me to do, and pray for workers for the other things, because there are so many abundant, overwhelming needs.

At this point the Lord let me know he had another challenge for me. He wanted me to learn to speak Thai.

CHAPTER NINE

LIFE, DEATH, AND PERSECUTION

For as the heavens are higher than the earth, so are my ways
higher than your ways,
and my thoughts than your thoughts.

Isaiah 55:9

B y this point I'm sure you're well aware of the difficulty
I have learning languages, particularly those that are so
different from English. Nevertheless, it was clear to me
that for ministry and personal growth I needed to be able to
converse in Thai at least as well as I could in Karen. The Lord
had impressed upon me that this was important, so as usual, I
believed that if He gave me the assignment, He would help me
complete it. This time I would have a little company. Shaune
and Shalise had also felt called to learn Thai, which I hoped
would be a big advantage. We would be able to study together
formally, and then practice amongst ourselves informally. I
was hopeful that this experience would be easier than learning
Karen, so the three of us found a private teacher and got to
work. I wish I could say that everything went smoothly, but
that wasn't the case. We studied for about one year with the
Thai teacher, but I was having my usual difficult time. I finally

had to admit that the only way I was going to become proficient in Thai would be to go to an established school, and the one we selected was in Bangkok. It seemed like the right thing to do, but then the Lord revealed to both our pastor and me that He didn't want Shalise living in Bangkok. This was a disappointment for me, but as always, we obeyed. Shaune and Shalise moved to Chiang Mai and I prepared to move to Bangkok alone. As it turned out, Chiang Mai was the place the Lord intended them to minister. They never came back down south, so we didn't continue working together. I was disappointed, but God had a different plan. He always knows the complete picture and our future—and its always best.

Although Shaune and Shalise had moved on, I had wonderful new company in my life. My son and daughter-in-law, Brad and Kristen, arrived to visit right before I moved to Bangkok. Even better, they found out she was pregnant right before they came. I was going to be a grandmother again! They had planned on visiting other countries, too, so had quit their jobs, sold everything, and stopped their insurance. The birth was going to have to be paid for with cash, so I suggested they have the baby in Thailand where the medical care is good and the costs are reasonable. We had a wonderful week together and then I moved to Bangkok to begin language school. They had my place in Hua Hin to themselves after I left, so they had a place to live while they reconsidered their plans. Traveling to other countries no longer seemed like a good idea with the baby due, so Brad decided to look for a teaching job. He was accepted for one in northeast Thailand. We weren't all together, but at least we were in the same country for a change.

As it turned out, Kristen wasn't the only one in my extended family getting ready to have a baby. My "Karen daughter" La Lay Sha was also pregnant, and due close to the same time as

Kristen. It was the first baby for both Kristen and La Lay Sha, so that made the whole thing all the more exciting. I completed my language school courses right before La Lay Sha was due, so I moved back to Hua Hin to be available. God had me right where He wanted me. Sadly, La Lay Sha's son was born with a serious heart defect. The hospital in Hua Hin was small and not equipped to handle his condition, so he was sent by ambulance to the closest hospital that had better facilities. In this case, better wasn't good enough. They didn't communicate with us and we couldn't see the baby. I decided that this wasn't going to do at all, so I called a private hospital in Bangkok and had the baby and parents transferred there by ambulance. Being in a well-equipped hospital was certainly better, but not the complete solution to the problem. The baby needed immediate surgery. The many doctors who examined the baby were very caring and sensitive with La Lay Sha and her husband, but they also didn't want to create false hope. The baby's heart was incomplete and there were risks involved with the surgery. They said he had a fifty-fifty chance, and if he lived, he would need many surgeries in the future.

There is an oppressive sadness that comes over one when a tiny, defenseless baby is in such a dire condition. We did what we always do during times of trial: we prayed. The decision of whether or not to have surgery was wrenching, and I left the choice to the parents. They decided it was the best choice and he was taken to the operating room, but he lived only a few hours after surgery. Because I still had a room in Bangkok, we had wonderful prayer support and people to help us. All was being prepared for the funeral and burial at the village as we drove back from Bangkok. His service was very simple and emotional. He was the first of our family at the Bible school and my first Karen grandchild that the Lord called home.

I stayed with them for a while, then the Lord clearly led me to go to Roi Et to be with Brad and Kristen right away when it was her time to deliver. Labor began that night and she had Gabriel the next day. I love listening to and obeying the Lord when He tells me what to do. Looking back, I can see that the Lord led me to go to the language school in Bangkok so I could finish my studies right before these two babies were born and be available for them.

One family rejoices and another family mourns. Many ask how God could allow such a thing to happen, but the answer is in the first book of the Bible. The world we live in is not the one God intended for us, but one that has become corrupt through sin. God is very clear that He will never leave us or forsake us. We don't understand His ways now, but some day we will.

❦

After fleeing in 1997, I kept getting letters from Sah Tweh, one of the students that I had supported at Beh Klaw Bible school. He kept asking me to come and visit him, but he left out an important detail: he didn't tell me where he was. He told me he was in Pa Dang village, which would have been helpful, except that Pa Dang village does not appear on any map. All I knew was that he was somewhere in a small village and I couldn't wander all over the country randomly looking for him. Finding him was going to be like solving a puzzle.

One of our former Ah Moe Mission School teachers, Theramu Paw Thweh, had gone up into the mountains of Chiang Mai to teach after we fled the Burmese Army. I heard that she had married a Thai pastor, but the story seemed very strange. The pastor, Reverend Nikorn, had lost his wife in an automobile accident about two years prior, and had also been involved in a serious accident a few years before when he fell off a cliff into a river and split his head open. That he survived was a miracle in itself, although he had some bad side effects which required people to help him with some of his everyday tasks of life. His friends decided that Theramu Paw Thweh would be the ideal person to do that. They arranged this marriage, they both agreed to it, and we heard from the sidelines that our Ah Moe Mission School teacher had married an "old Thai pastor." Everybody was talking about it in a negative way. I wanted to find her and learn the true story. Was it a good one, or a bad one? What really happened? I don't trust rumors, so I kept praying that I would find her. I had found her a few years earlier in the mountains above Chiang Mai, so I figured that would be the best place to start. While searching and asking questions I found out they were living in Ratchaburi, which is in the south, so I headed back down south again. Success! By God's grace I was able to find them. When I arrived in Ratchaburi, I telephoned them and they came and picked me up. They were very gracious. I stayed with them then, and many times in the future. And that, finally, led me to Sah Tweh.

Theramu Paw Thweh and her husband knew Sah Tweh was trying to find me, and better still, they actually knew where Pa Dang village was. They offered to take me to him, so off we went. When we reached the village, we stopped at the house of one of the elders who Reverend Nikorn knew, and he summoned Sah Tweh to come and meet me. It was a happy reunion. Sah Tweh had something on his mind besides just seeing me again. He wanted to know if I could help send him back to Beh Klaw refugee camp so he could attend the English Bible school course. Americans take traveling and education for granted, but in parts of the world like this it's not nearly as simple as what we are accustomed to. He needed some assistance and he knew I could help.

Sah Tweh was the leader on the last evangelism trip that we went on from Ah Moe Mission School in December of 1996 and he is gifted. I knew that as he learned English, the Lord would use him even more. He is very bold and speaks straight out for the Lord. If he sees somebody in sin, he confronts them, tells them, and prays for them. He is a person who I believed would be worth investing in. As Paul says of Timothy, to train up faithful men. Standing in agreement with him was one thing, but getting on with the practical aspects of his goal was something else.

Sah Tweh has been serving the Lord as a teacher at the Bible school in Pa Dang village. The principal, Paw Gay, told me that the Lord had given him a vision to start a Bible school. Again, this would not be a particularly difficult chore in the United States, but we had recently fled from the Burmese Army and there was still fear and uncertainty when he had started the school, with only two students in the first year. By the end of the next year, he had ten students and needed another teacher. He found Sah Tweh in the Tham Hin refugee camp and he agreed to go with him and teach, but now we wanted to take him away. We discussed the problem and agreed that it would be fair if we were to find another teacher to replace Sah Tweh while he went back to school. I now had another piece of the puzzle to search for.

I went to Beh Klaw Bible school and talked to my Karen daughter, Juty, who was going to graduate that year, and asked her to pray about teaching in Pa Dang. She wasn't against the idea, but there was another consideration. Her boyfriend Htoo Gay was also interested in going, but had been chosen by the Australian Baptist mission to go to a Bible school in Australia after he graduated. This was a very good opportunity for him, so this decision was not to be taken lightly, and we decided to wait and see what the situation was after he graduated. After they prayed together, they believed that the Lord wanted her to go and teach at this Bible school. It was a perfect opportunity to go back down south where there needed to be some light and some fruit, exactly as the Lord had put on my heart, so I got really excited about it. We had confirmation of the decision because at graduation Htoo Gay found out he was not able to go to Australia because the Thai authorities would not allow anybody without legal papers to leave the country. However, he had caught the attention of one of the other Karen reverends, who had appointed him to be the youth director of the whole Mae Sot area. This was another great opportunity not to be taken lightly. Htoo Gay talked to me about it and then asked me to talk to that reverend. I told him the vision, about the Bible school in the south, and he said he would talk to Htoo Gay. After their conversation, the reverend readily agreed for him to go and teach. The Lord gave them a clear "go" to come down and teach at the Bible school in the south. They married first, then we left the next day. We were all really excited.

For many people, the world is very small. They live and die in their village or town and that is about as much of the world as they ever see. So it was for Htoo Gay. He had no idea how far away Pa Dang was. I'm sure he felt the way we do when we travel to another state. We kept going, and going, and going and he was amazed at how far he had traveled. Finally, after sixteen hours, we reached our destination. While he and Juty were happy and excited about their new opportunity, they were also cautious. In the biblical sense they "spied out the land" for two years to ensure that the Bible school was based on solid Christian principles and to seek God's assurance that this is where he wanted them. There were a few other issues. People talk. There were some questions and accusations about things the principal had done twenty years ago. They were worth examining. When we spoke to him about our concerns, and asked many others to speak to him, he said he had repented and changed. All believed that these weaknesses in his life where the same weaknesses we all face. We felt comfortable proceeding.

As our faith grew, so did the school. The principal, Paw Gay, decided he wanted to buy land in another village and build the school there. I had counsel from many respected friends, including Herman Janzen, a longtime missionary in the country. Herman ran a foundation from Chiang Mai, and was always interested in projects that would improve life for the population. Herman believed in this project, and wrote a proposal for their mission organization to help. The Lord miraculously gave us a "go ahead" to build the Bible school in Pa La U village. None of the land there had any legal deeds. The mission organization in Germany sent the funds to purchase the land and a truck to get us started. We talked to my Karen children and the others from Ah Moe Mission School, who were studying at Beh Klaw, and asked who would be willing to commit to at least two years at this Bible school. They all agreed. As soon as they graduated, they came to teach and everything was progressing wonderfully for a year.

Then the persecution started.

It was amazing. Nonbelievers in Pa La U village came against us. Christians came against us. You would have thought we were trying to disrupt their entire society, not educate children. It was started by non-Christians who were jealous of the school and "Christians" who were not walking with the Lord, who also were jealous and wanted to have the land and the buildings. This has happened in Thailand many times. The Thai authorities come in and they close down the school, and the missionaries have to leave. I had heard about this, and many people had warned me. Herman was our answer man. He knew people personally who this had happened to, but he also totally believed in this project, that it was God's and no one would steal it from us. Every time I called him or met with him, he said, "Don't worry. God will work it out." I just had to rest in that because he's the one who's been in Thailand for so long and knows that culture and government. I trusted God to speak through him for everything.

Herman, who arranged the funding for the school, came down to an area near us for a holiday with his wife, Margaret, and I had invited them to the school for Thanksgiving—an American Thanksgiving celebration, complete with turkey and all the trimmings. While they were there, we had a Thanksgiving service and Herman shared Psalm 46:10, "Be still and know that I am God; I will be exalted among the nations, I will be exalted in the earth." I also shared some of my concerns about what was going on at the school and in the community with Herman. Much of the trouble centered around a non-Christian teacher who sometimes taught the Thai language at the school. He had been meddling in the affairs of the school and now wanted to move on campus with a woman he was living with and her son. After sharing my concerns with Herman, Paw Gay took him to meet this Thai village teacher. Everything exploded after that. Ulterior motives were exposed, and the Thai teacher and Paw Gay came to the school to explain that if we were to continue to go on as we were, they would bring the police to the school on the next Tuesday and have it closed, since it didn't have any land deed and couldn't legally belong to us.

The village didn't have telephone service, but in a terrific example of His timing, the Lord had just provided a satellite phone for us by an unexpected supporter. Praise the Lord.

Herman and his wife had gone to Prachuabkirikan, but the satellite phone enabled me to reach him at the Christian guesthouse there and tell him what was going on. He asked me to come down to Prachuabkirikan to meet with him and the head of the adult rural education and other Thai officers. The Lord provided a Thai reverend, who was head of a Bible school in Prachuabkirikan, to help and encourage us. He provided everybody and everything we needed. After the meetings, we thought things were okay. The resistance and deception had all been exposed. Phone calls were made from district offices to the village officials telling them not to bother us. We thought things were better. We were wrong. Things actually got worse. Some people in the village were even more upset than before and continued to come against us. To make things even worse, outside people in the districts and provinces got involved. There were so many meetings to go to and forms to be written up it was enough to make our heads spin. It was as though we were trying to take over the country. Slowly and laboriously, we wrote our proposals for the school and why we wanted to build it.

My participation in this project was well known, so I had to be at one of the meetings. Village leaders, people from surrounding villages, teachers, and an assortment of concerned parties were all there. At one point, I had to give my testimony of why I was even involved in this school and how I got started in it. They wanted me to speak in Karen, the language that had challenged me for years. I personally lived through what I needed to say, so it would be clear in my mind, but communicating it effectively in Karen was not easy for me. However, that turned out to be one of those anointed times, and from the first word until the last, the Lord gave me total clarity. Afterward, everybody was so excited that I was able to say it in Karen. It really encouraged them to know that I have a heart for them, even those who were against me. They could see that I love the Karen enough to learn their language, to live with them, and to live like them. They all took a vote at the end of this meeting of who wanted to move the Thai language lessons away from our campus to the village school, or some other location. It was unanimous that they would move it off of our school campus. That was the Lord's victory!

Another part of this victory was how the Lord used Reverend Nikorn in the meeting. Before the meeting, he prayed for wisdom and the Lord gave him the ten conditions of the Thai mission umbrella for Christians. These ten conditions are written in the front of a book for all people in Thailand. It is written so that no one can persecute a Christian for their religion. That one cannot come against Christians. That one cannot take anything away from Christians. He started the meeting in prayer, then read these ten things. It silenced everybody. There really wasn't anything else they could say. After he spoke, I gave my involvement testimony in Karen, a Thai officer spoke, then they voted to move the Thai language lessons off campus.

It's very hard in Thailand for Thai people to "lose face." But it was clear to everybody at that meeting that the Thai teacher needed to leave the school. After he left, it was revealed to me, by others, that Paw Gay was involved in selling idols. That is a sin and I hadn't known of his involvement. This was God's way of removing the sin from our Bible school, and he voluntarily left. The Lord used this man as His tool to get the land and school arranged, then exposed his sin. God can use any of us, not because we're wonderful, not because we're good, not because we're godly, but because He chooses to. This is a lesson the Lord continuously shows me to keep me humble. He has not chosen me because there is anything good in me, but because

He has chosen to choose me. It's His choice. I can be the evilest person in the world, yet He will choose me for His purposes. I can never take pride in anything that I do because I know 100 percent that it's all God, none of me. I love being reminded of this and I love staying in this position because God gets all the glory. There is no credit that I can take for anything.

While all of this was going on, I understood nothing. All of the meetings were in the Thai language and the only Thai native involved was the village headman. In the midst of all of this paperwork and confusion, the Lord sent Reverend Nikorn to sort things out for us. He was not involved when we bought the land, nor at the time of our first threat, because we did not know him well enough yet. However, by the time we needed him, we knew him well and God used him to get our school registered properly. Htoo Gay and Paw Gay didn't know how to do the paperwork, and I certainly didn't, but within twenty-four hours Reverend Nikorn had everything established legally. He was a total answer to prayer. This is only one of the many examples that I can tell you how God, from day one, has been working everything together. The people that He has brought into my life, the Karen He has brought into my life. Why? I don't know, but He knows. He arranges absolutely everything that we need when we need it.

The opposition slowly died down. Then the school was able to go forward and evangelize openly, clearly, freely. Htoo Gay became the head of the Bible school at twenty-seven years old. I saw God choosing this man, and bringing him here. He knew nothing about the spiritual bareness in the southern part of the Karen area. Now he knows, he sees, he understands, and he's committed to helping these people in the south spiritually, to know who Jesus is and His love for them. That they would come to know Him, love Him, give their lives to Him, receive

His salvation and eternal life. He is such a wonderful gift from God.

Another wonderful part of Htoo Gay's story is that Juty had another boyfriend at Ah Moe Mission School, and Daniel Zu, who was the principal then, did not like his character. I didn't know him that well, but what I knew of him I also didn't like. I told Juty that we didn't think he was who God had chosen for her. She said she thought if some boy had chosen her, then it must automatically be God's will. Many Karen believe this. This is part of discipleship, and why I believe the Lord chose these particular children to be in my home. I did not choose any of them. I knew none of them beforehand. He handpicked these children, and brought them to me. I know that He chose them for the purpose to be who they are now, and where they are now. This was God's plan from the beginning, which none of us knew anything about. We thought we were all going to be living in the jungle forever. None of us knew ahead of time we would be fleeing into Thailand. But God knew it, and God prepared years ago for this very purpose, for this very day. It's so exciting to see it all come about. To see the children He has chosen be obedient to Him, to follow Him, and see Him bless them. Juty ended up breaking off that relationship when she went to Bible school, and God provided her with Htoo Gay, who God has anointed to be a Karen spiritual leader in the south. She is a very understanding and lovely wife. They have two daughters and a son. I am excited for them and pray that they will continue to be obedient to Him, and humble before Him, so He can use them and glorify Himself through them for many years to come.

Because of the opposition and persecution at the Thai Karen Bible School, the students lessened, but all the teachers chose to stay. That was another miracle. When the non-Christian Thai teacher came and said if we continued on, he would arrange for the police to come and close down the school, Paw Gay, the principal at that time, said, "I will have nothing to do with this school until this situation is all cleared up. You do not know me, and I do not know you."

Htoo Gay followed suit and said, "I also will go away. I will leave." I looked at him and saw Satan. I knew at that point what a mighty spiritual battle this was. I looked at him in amazement, yet the Lord gave me strength to say, "You all can leave. I don't care who leaves, but I will stay. I prayed, and we've prayed since the beginning. We believe this is God's Bible school, and I will stick with God's will to the end." Then I went to bed and prayed. I had no idea, but that gave so much strength and conviction to everybody who was there. The next day Htoo Gay apologized to everybody, and said he was wrong. God convicted him that he would be wrong to leave, that he was staying. Every single one of our teachers stayed. It is all praise to God.

Also, by Saw Tweh's staying, he started a twenty-four-hour prayer time. Everybody's faith was shaken, but all the teachers and some of the students stayed and prayed. Because of this, so many grew in maturity. It was so exciting to see them grow in their faith. They now knew personally that the Lord is with them and that He will continue to be with them, to lead them and guide them to do what He wants them to do, and where He wants them to be in the future. Some will stay at the Bible school; some will go out and plant churches in other villages. Some will be evangelists. God has a special purpose and a special plan for each and every one and He will reveal His plan to them in His perfect way, and in His perfect timing. I'm excited to see what the Lord will do in each of their lives in the future.

I also thank God for Herman's faith through this whole thing. His faith never wavered. He believed from the beginning that God would see us through this, that He would be glorified, and He would establish His school in the south. I praise Him and thank Him for His faithfulness. On April 20, 2003 the Lord used the staff and students to glorify Himself, singing and preaching about His resurrection. They began to learn dramas, and to invite villagers from both near and far to attend. Now the churches are all united, working together. They have prayer and Bible study meetings every month. These churches were divided before, but the Lord chose this team to unite them. We pray that this will be an example for other churches who come, for them to evangelize in each of their villages every year on Resurrection Day.

If I look at the beginning from December 1985 until now and see the progress, I'm totally amazed. None of us would have had any idea what the Lord was going to do. From the beginning of not knowing any of the culture, the language, the food, nothing, to not having electricity and the hot weather, to what God has built today, I just marvel . . . though I shouldn't . . . and thank Him for everything He has done.

CHAPTER TEN

IN THE SHADOW OF DEATH

You will keep him in perfect peace, whose mind is stayed on You,
because he trusts in You.

Isaiah 26:3,4

What is it like to serve the Lord as a missionary? For the first three decades of my life, that was a question I never asked, in fact, it was the furthest question from my mind. When I first went to serve the Karen people, filled with trepidation and uncertainty, I had no idea what it would be like to live as a missionary overseas. Then, in January of 2002, I suddenly found myself on the brink of knowing what it was like to die like one.

Despite the knowledge that God had called me to help the Karen people, who have become so special to me, in the beginning my work was filled with trials and disappointments. Just because He calls us it doesn't mean He is going to make it easy. I thought I would serve as best I could for six months—maybe a year— and then go back to my life in Southern California. I had no idea I would still be here. It amazes me. I never had missions on my mind. I didn't understand what being a missionary was. I really knew no missionaries, other than one friend who was serving in Taiwan. As I was preparing to leave for Thailand, I prayed for her. That was the extent of my involvement. In fact, I knew so little about the whole thing that I wouldn't have known anything else to do for her. I had never read a book on missions until after the Lord sent me to the Karen. He enabled me, miraculously, to do each thing He asked me to do, step by step. Even after the first six months when I went back to the States, I still was not thinking long-term. But, they kept asking me to return and I had a burning desire to return to the village and people God had so recently and unexpectedly put on my heart. Before I left for Thailand, neither I nor anyone in my church knew who the Karen were. Even today, after all these years and many trips back to the States to speak in churches, there are still very few people who understand the Karen and their plight. I pray for them, as the Lord continues to keep me here. I am humbled that He chose me, although this task was at times more harrowing than I could ever have dreamed. December 2001 was one of those times.

In January of 2002 I had spent the early part of the month evangelizing with the Karen as usual, going from village to village, celebrating the Christmas season with them. This wonderful time of the year is always festive, with the Bible school students putting on dramas, singing, and spreading the Gospel. At the Thai Karen Bible Institute (now called the Pa La U Discipleship Center), we celebrated with an outreach for all the villages to come to hear the Gospel and have an opportunity to accept the Lord. It was exceptionally busy, but a time of happiness and excitement.

Following December's crowded holiday schedule, I was invited to the northernmost Karen refugee camp, Mae Ra Moe, for Pastor Robert Tweh's annual Thanksgiving service. He celebrates every January to thank the Lord for His blessings the previous year and pray ahead for the new year. As head of the refugee camps in the north, Pastor Tweh, had invited me to come to the service many times over the years, but I never had time to go. December was always exhausting, and Mae Ra Moe refugee camp is far away from Beh Klaw refugee camp, where the Bible school is located. But Pastor Robert's wife had just passed away the November before, so I decided to make the trip to be an encouragement to him. I went up to Beh Klaw camp first, and transportation arrangements were made for many of us to go into Mae Ra Moe camp. For many years I had heard stories about the terrible road to the camp; that it is an extremely difficult, rough, tough road up and down mountains. In the States, a rough road might have a few potholes. In Thailand, a rough road is barely a road at all. People who had made the trip before unanimously agreed it was miserable, and that was the main reason I had not gone in the past. But this year was different. I wanted to be there for pastor Robert, so I decided I could put up with a little additional discomfort. *I'd certainly had plenty of it during my time as a missionary*, I thought, *so what was a little more?*

Joining me on the trip was Sah Tweh and another student, Lweh Htoo, who I was sending for medical training in Mae Sot. Our mode of transportation was really crude and hard to describe. We had to be in the back of a huge, ten-wheel truck. The road was every bit as bad as we had been warned, even worse than I had imagined. Bumps and holes in the road launched the truck in every which direction. There were only four of us in the back of this huge, empty truck trying unsuccessfully to stand or sit without anything to hold onto.

We bounced in every which direction, to the left, then the right, and then on top of each other. It was like traveling in a washing machine. And the trip was long—eight hours in total— five of which were an absolutely horrid experience on that dirt road. As soon as we arrived, I gratefully laid down on the wooden dorm room floor and slept soundly. However, the next day I did enjoy the Thanksgiving celebration and seeing many people that I hadn't seen for many years. I was really glad that I went.

As always, the Lord is faithful to provide what we need. After the event was over with, friends on a mission team from Alaska decided to help me and take me out on a different road. I had heard that this road was better, so Sah Tweh and I optimistically went out with them. It was better in the sense that it had fewer bumps and holes and we were sitting on seats inside a small Suzuki, but it was almost entirely winding, twisting, and turning down the mountainsides like a crumpled strand of spaghetti. By the time I got to the bottom I was quite sick. They had to stop and I lost everything inside of me. I'll leave out the details, since I'm sure you can imagine them. I had never been carsick in my life, and never want to be again.

After resting long enough for my insides to properly collect themselves, I felt a little bit better and we went with the team from Alaska to the hotel where they were staying in Chiang Mai. It was a very nice hotel and they were absolutely wonderful to me. They paid for us to stay there for two nights, then they paid our way to fly back down south. Sah Tweh had fun staying with the guys on the missionary team, experiencing many new things, like ice skating! I was more than happy just to have a much-needed rest.

I was still very fatigued from two months of strenuous activity, but was feeling better when we arrived back in the south. Then Jeff Jackson, the head of Shepherd's Staff, the mission facilitator that sends my monthly support, arrived. I drove him to the TKBI Bible school in Pa La U village and thought I was doing fine while he was there, but as soon as he left, I drove back to my place in Hua Hin city and collapsed. I ended up with a fever, bronchitis, an eye infection, and eventually a very painful case of shingles. I guess I was really worn out; it finally all caught up with me. To put it bluntly, I was a mess. I called the Bible school and two girls came out and stayed with me with the intention of helping me, but they took one look at me and immediately took me to the hospital so I could get proper treatment. For two months—which seemed much longer—I really wasn't very strong. After I had gotten over the shingles and the infections, I was much better, but was still tired. La Lay Sha continued to stay with me and help me, which was a much-appreciated blessing.

By March I was feeling much better, but not ready to travel anywhere. This is the time of year when students at the Bible school in Beh Klaw refugee camp graduate. This graduation has always been very important to me and I attended every year, because that is where I sent my kids. This particular year I had not sent anyone who was graduating, but there was another student with whom I was close and she wanted me to be there for her. Also, Pastor Robert Tweh, wanted to meet with me about arranging and organizing help for the internally displaced people (IDPs) in the south. He called and I promised him that I would go, but I was still quite tired. Common sense kicked in and I arranged with Htoo Gay, the head of TKBI Bible school, to meet with him for me, and to explain to the girl who was graduating that I really wasn't feeling up to traveling and needed to rest. Everything was arranged, so I would stay at my place in Hua Hin until I had fully recovered my health. That decision didn't last long.

Max, the well digger from Australia, called and asked me if I was going. I told him no. Well, he didn't take no for an answer and kept asking me over and over in several different ways. I told him I was tired and recuperating and didn't want to face the difficulty of traveling a long way in a car. He was persistent and said he wanted to take a break from his work and felt it was important to him to visit the Karen, especially when they were graduating. While I admired Max's desire to be a blessing to the young graduates, his good intentions weren't going to cure my health. It just didn't seem wise to me, but he continued to discuss it. He said he would like to come and bless anybody who would like to go up there to the graduation and he would do all of the driving so I could relax along the way. He was positive it wouldn't be hard for anybody. I asked La Lay Sha, who was caring for me and listening to the conversation, to pray. He finally wore me down enough for me to consider it, but I set some stipulations. I didn't want to rush on this trip, so I told him he would have to get a flight that would arrive in Bangkok by Wednesday so he could get to Hua Hin, and get a very good night's sleep before our departure on Thursday. If he could do that I would go. If not, I was going to stay right where I was.

He called me back in about an hour. He had called a travel agent he had never used before, and they got him the last seat on an airplane that would get him to Bangkok on time. He would arrive at exactly noon on Wednesday. Somehow, I hadn't thought he would be able to pull that off. I looked at La Lay Sha, we talked, prayed, and decided it must be God's will. I had set specific requirements, and God fulfilled them all. That was obvious. Perhaps God wanted me to go and see Robert Tweh myself to organize what we needed to do for the IDPs. I decided that if it was God's will, I would be obedient.

Max arrived on time and got a good night's sleep in town, and when we left Thursday morning I actually felt pretty well and rested. Heh Ney Htoo would be making the trip with us, and I felt good about that. There was just one small thing that bothered me. We would be traveling in my "new" car that I had purchased two weeks earlier.

I had been driving an older Suzuki for several years, but when I got shingles, I couldn't use the gear shift anymore, it was just too painful. I had the same problem with the non-power steering; it suddenly became a great effort in my physical condition. I had actually been praying about my car situation for over a year. That may seem strange to some people, but as a missionary it's very important that I be a good steward of the money I receive. I carefully budget to take care of my necessities, but luxuries are excluded. That's fine with me. The question had become, is another car, with an automatic transmission, a necessity or a luxury? I consulted with my trusted spiritual brothers and sisters. In the end, the answer was obvious to us all. At my age and in my physical condition, the Suzuki was just too hard to drive. I would need to get another car.

With some assistance from my friends, I went car shopping and ended up buying a nine-year-old Toyota Corolla. I had another person check it out to make sure it was a good buy, and a good car. I'm a missionary not a mechanic. I was trying to do it carefully, and not get ahead of God. I thought I had made the right purchase, but as soon as I brought the car home, I wasn't comfortable with it. I have to be honest. I knew I would never drive it into a Karen village. It was an older car and it was not an expensive car, but it looked expensive. I have the mind-set and belief not to live above those I serve. For me to drive into a Karen village, or a refugee camp, in a car that looked expensive bothered me. I knew the car was inexpensive, but they wouldn't know. I realize that most people wouldn't have to justify buying a nine-year-old Toyota, but I believe it's critical for a missionary to meet the people they serve at their own level. A nine-year-old Toyota that appeared fancy was beyond the means of the

Karen that I serve, and that concerned me. I had been struggling with the purchase for two weeks and asking myself if I really needed that particular car, but when it came time for the trip to the Bible school graduation, it was what I had. It troubled me enough that I thought I might leave the car parked when we got close to the camp and enter on public transportation. That may seem a bit silly, but as events transpired, the car would be the least of my problems.

Before we left, the man who had helped me buy the car found out we were driving it to Beh Klaw, which is about a twelve-hour journey, and said, "You're driving the new car?" I said, "Yes." He looked surprised, but didn't say anything more. I let it pass because he was the one who had checked the car out, so I thought it was a good sturdy car. I thought maybe that was what he was thinking, so his comment didn't concern me. We left on Thursday morning and stopped by Reverend Nikorn and Theramu Paw Thweh's house, to see them on the way. I remember Reverend Nikorn saying, "You're driving that car all the way up to Mae Sot?" I said, "Yes." He also didn't say anything else. Since then, both of them have said that they had a check in their spirits about the car, but neither one of them said anything to me about it, so I didn't pick up on it. We went on our way.

Several hours later, when we neared the town of Nakhon Sawan, about halfway there, I was wearing out. I told Max that I was tired and didn't want to go any farther. I wanted to stop in the next town and sleep there. What I didn't say was that I wanted to sleep in a *hotel*. We did end up sleeping in Nakhon Sawan, but in a hospital. I definitely got a good rest; I got two months' rest in an intensive care unit.

To this day, I don't know exactly what happened. Sometime after I said I wanted to sleep in Nakhon Sawan, we got into an accident. I have no recollection of the experience. I praise God for His grace that He is not allowing me to remember the accident so I don't have any flashbacks. What I do remember is waking up in the wreckage of my car, screaming in pain. I realized that my seat was flat back—that it had broken—and Heh Ney Htoo was sitting next to me praying fervently. I continued screaming, and he said, "It's going to be okay. It's going to be okay." I remember pleading for aspirin, and hearing somebody that seemed far away saying, "No! No! That's not good for her." I told him, "Give it to me anyway!" so he did. Then I passed out.

I remember riding in a vehicle, and I remember them pulling into what I assume was a hospital. I did not open my eyes. I remember them driving back out again because the hospital wouldn't take me. Why I was rejected I don't know. They took me to another hospital. I remember going in and crying out for them to help me. The pain was unbearable. This was all complicated by the fact that we were in a foreign country where most of the hospital staff didn't understand English and none of us spoke Thai. In my condition, I was not in the presence of mind to speak Thai anyway. I kept trying to communicate with them in English, but to no avail. I remember people walking by and not even looking at me. I was crying out, then passing out. The only other thing I remember is being taken to the x-ray room. It was either on my way there, or on the way back, that Max passed me, also on a rolling bed. He said, "This is not exactly what you had in mind for sleeping in Nakhon Sawan, is it?" I was in too much pain to appreciate his sense of humor.

They finished the x-rays and took me back to the emergency ward. I remember Heh Ney Htoo sitting next to my bed. When they took me away from the accident in the vehicle, I wondered if I would ever see him again. Despite my own dire circumstances, I was really worried about him. Seeing him gave me a measure of peace amidst the pain and turmoil. I was thankful and could rest because he was there. I remember telling him to call La Lay Sha and my kids at Pa La U village to let them know what happened. I thought I showed him how to use the phone, but apparently not. Nevertheless, somehow word got out and within twelve hours Htoo Gay, Curt (the one who checked my car out), Mabel Htoo (a nurse at our school), and all kinds of people were there with me. I don't remember anything else; I only know the story of what they told me. They said I pled with them, "Don't leave me here. I will die. Can you find a private hospital?" They inquired and there "just happened" to be, by God's grace, a private hospital on the next street. They moved me there immediately.

The other thing Heh Ney Htoo told me was that I kept saying, "Don't worry. God is in control." It blesses me so much that I knew that when I was in so much pain. I remember being wheeled into a private hospital on a bed and a man coming up to me and saying, "Don't worry about anything. I'm a Christian. We'll take good care of you now that you're here." Then they took me up to their intensive care unit. I don't remember too much other than screaming when they sliced my arm to do some kind of test. Medical people would understand that. I remember being in a lot of pain and I remember more x-rays being taken, but I don't remember them telling me I needed to go into exploratory surgery. That surgery turned out to be a mixed blessing.

I was in and out of consciousness and in a blur of pain medication, but when I awoke after my surgery, my daughter Shelly was there. She had endured a frightening phone call about me, an emergency plane ride from America to Bangkok, a taxi to an unknown hospital somewhere in a city she'd never been to, all while not knowing if I was dead or alive. But by God's grace she got to me. It was such a wonderful blessing.

She stayed with me, along with Mabel Htoo, who I had sent to medical training in Mae Sot, and Moonlight, who had finished medical training in the jungle and graduated from Bible school in Beh Klaw. All three of them were there and helped take care of Max, who had two or three broken ribs, and me. Heh Ney Htoo was fine, even though his head shattered the rear window, so he went on to the Bible school graduation.

The doctor told me to eat anything that I wanted. Personally, I thought that was very strange, but I figured he's the doctor, I'm not, so I'd better do what he says, and I was very hungry, so I ate everything they provided. That seemed fine—right up until the minute when my intestines ruptured again. A drain hole patch they put in me was becoming wet. I showed Shelly and she called the nurses. They said that was normal, but it concerned me, so I opened it up a bit and undigested food poured out. Shelly called the nurses again and they confirmed the obvious. "No, that's not all right," they shouted and ran off to get a doctor for me. My first surgeon, who was a Christian and elder in his church, was at a conference in China, but he had checked in on me that morning before he left because he was worried about me. He was already gone when the intestine ruptured, but he had arranged for another doctor to take care of me in his absence. That doctor came, took one look at me, and realized I needed surgery again. The first surgery had been exploratory. I was in a great deal of pain, but the x-rays didn't show anything wrong, so they had to go in and take a look. Once they had me opened up, they immediately saw that my intestines were ruptured—as were my lungs—injuries from the seat belt. They repaired the tears in my organs but, unfortunately, the intestinal closure wasn't secure. When I started eating it let go and my condition became critical. Once again, Shelly got some news she didn't want to hear.

It was obvious that I needed surgery to bypass my stomach, but the doctor wasn't optimistic. He told Shelly to discuss my funeral wishes with me, because he felt it was unlikely I would survive the surgery. I was in a bad spot. If he left me as I was, I would die. If he performed the surgery, I would probably die. Shelly and I had the conversation, and I was actually full of unexplainable joy and peace. I knew I would go to be with Jesus. I asked her to keep my funeral simple. I requested she give me to the Karen, who would make a box, dig a hole in the ground, and praise God that I was with Jesus. She understood and she accepted my wishes, which was a blessing for me.

At that point, death seemed like a needed release for me. I prayed and, because I was in so much pain, asked the Lord, "Please take me home." But He said, "No." He showed me a vision of being in this very plain, gray area, kind of like an alley with tall, gray buildings. All I could see were high gray walls and gray streets. Far away was a huge, long gate with bright lights behind it, and it was closed. That's how I knew that the Lord had other plans for me. He was not opening the gates for me at that time. I remember telling Him I couldn't handle the pain. He asked if I trusted Him. I said I did. Then He said, "Okay let's go." I went into surgery, came back out, in a lot of pain, but I was alive. The doctor told me, "We cannot properly take care of you here. You need to go to a good hospital in Bangkok or Chiang Mai." Traveling was certainly the last thing I wanted to do, but I understood and appreciated his professional opinion and concern for me. I said I would like to go to Chiang Mai, where I had many missionary friends, as well as lots of Karen for support and prayer. There was no time to waste. "You have to travel today, because tomorrow will be more dangerous," he warned me.

They put me into an ambulance. It's about a six-hour drive from Nakhon Sawan to Chiang Mai, but we had an un-expected delay. The ambulance broke down. At that time my blood pressure went down to 40/20. Shelly couldn't believe it. They checked it again. Still 40/20. I was coherent (probably not too coherent) enough that I knew what was going on. I remember them calling for another ambulance to come from the hospital in Chiang Mai while they periodically tried to restart the ambulance I was in. After what seemed like an eternity, the ambulance from Chiang Mai finally arrived. With my dangerously low blood pressure, Shelly was afraid that just transferring me from one vehicle to another would kill me. She pleaded with them to try and start the ambulance I was in one more time. They did and it started right up. They didn't have to move me and I went ahead in the same ambulance. God's miracle. One of the many through this whole ordeal.

I arrived at Chiang Mai Ram Two Hospital where a doctor was expecting me. He was my second surgeon's professor and definitely God's provision for me. He's a wonderful doctor and took very good care of me, admitting me to the intensive care unit immediately. As the days progressed, my condition was erratic. It went from an emergency, to a praise, then a praise to an emergency, day by day. It was a roller-coaster experience for two solid months. My lungs would fill up with fluid, and they would have to drain them. One time after draining them, fluid just came flowing and bubbling out of my mouth. I lost consciousness. I just remember coughing and this stuff just started coming up. I had to have four blood transfusions and I was on a ventilator. The story goes on and on, and there's a whole set of emails that Shelly, in her faithfulness, wrote every day to update people on my condition and request them to praise or to pray. Every praise email she sent would initiate scores of praise emails coming back, and every emergency email would initiate scores of prayer emails coming back. It went on and on like that. Every email that was sent to me, I relished. It was one of the main things that kept me going, knowing that people were praying for me all over the world. In fact, I was amazed at the number of people who heard about my situation and were praying for me. God is truly all over the entire universe. People that I will never meet until I get to heaven were praying for me. I am so grateful for every single one of them.

I wasn't able to concentrate when people read the Bible to me. What got me through was listening to Christian praise songs on a cassette player. As long as I kept my focus on the Lord, and all the wonderful promises in His Word through music, I had His peace. As soon as the tapes stopped, I thought about my pain. Mabel Htoo, Moonlight, and my daughter Shelly each had eight-hour shifts and the girls were constantly starting the tapes over and over again, even all through the night. I am so thankful for their faithfulness and care.

After two months in the ICU, I was finally able to get off of the ventilator and be moved to a regular room, but I was still on oxygen and a feeding tube. As you can imagine, with my erratic physical condition, pain, and medication, I can't remember all the details. Looking back on it now, that might be good. My treatment went on and on, and in the end, there was no place to put another IV needle in me. I finally asked them to please take out all the tubes; I wanted to try to survive without them. My grandson, Trevor, was celebrating his birthday on May 12th, and Shelly needed to get back home to her family—she'd been away for two months already—and I really wanted to go with her. Despite all that was happening, I felt God's peace as

I prepared to leave on May 10th for the trip back to the States where we would be together for Mother's Day and Trevor's birthday. To make the trip, though, I needed to know I could survive without all those tubes, especially the feeding tube. The nutritionist was against it, but finally agreed to remove it to see what would happen. It was very difficult and painful to eat just soft food, but I was very motivated to recover, get on with my life, and spend time with my family. I prayed and did my best. I didn't gain as much weight as the doctor wanted me to, but he gave me his cautious clearance to leave the hospital and fly to the States. There were other problems. I had to learn to walk again in one week, use a wheelchair, a walker, and go to physical therapy to learn to care for myself again. My stomach had shrunk. I could eat very, very little and it was painful.

The Karen came often to sing and pray for me. My missionary friends came and prayed. It was such a blessing in the midst of a lot of pain, but a deeply appreciated blessing. God showed Himself true through everybody that came. There were so many wonderful prayers. The pastor from the Chiang Mai Community Church came, he prayed and brought communion. Just one blessing after another. I'm so thankful for everybody who gave their blood. I'm so thankful for everything everyone did.

The man, Bill Goei, who gave the funding for building both Ah Moe Mission School and Thai Karen Bible Institute, sent a representative, flowers, and money for first-class tickets to get us to the United States. Missionaries that I know don't fly first class, and I had certainly never done so before, so I was sorry I couldn't really enjoy the flight. But it was God's provision, in that I could lie flat and sleep the entire flight. Shelly was able to get me from one plane to another, and watched me as I struggled to get up and down the stairs of the Boeing 747, where our seats were upstairs. The Lord enabled me to do whatever I needed to do. I was glad to get where I needed to go. Coming back to America was really different. It was another culture adjustment for me, but everybody was really sweet and kind, and helped so much.

But perhaps the greatest feeling of all was the knowledge that that God wasn't done with me yet.

CHAPTER ELEVEN

TRIALS

The angel of the Lord encamps all around those who fear Him,
and delivers them.

Psalm 34:7

Some people think that being called by God to serve Him on the mission field is a very glamorous, easy thing to do. They think that being sent to an exotic location to work with people of different, interesting cultures is almost like being on vacation. If you've read this far in the book you know that's not true. It is just like being in our own country serving the Lord, day by day, step by step. It is hard, very hard. Being a pastor anywhere requires great commitment. Their congregations tend to believe that they should be available seven days a week twenty-four hours a day, and many are in times of crisis, but pastors are also human. They want to have a little time to themselves and with their families. People sometimes forget that. Being on the mission field is actually double the work because we also need to serve the people in our own countries by thanking them for their support, sending emails, communicating with them, and going back to visit them. The people back home who support us are providing a vital contribution to the salvation and discipling of the indigenous peoples in the missionary field country. They support us because they care a great deal about spreading the Gospel. Most cannot travel across the world to do it themselves, but they gladly do it through us by providing the resources we need. Naturally, they want to know how we're doing. How many have been saved? How many young people have gone to Bible school? How many new churches have been built? They are eager to know the fruits of their gifts and it is up to us to communicate the facts to them. That becomes a second job for the missionary. Sending pictures, newsletters, and praise reports is not just communication, it's also a blessing to our supporters to show them that their faith and commitment are having tangible results. Like the local pastor who hopes to have Monday off to relax or engage in a hobby, we like to have a little time off, too, but sometimes the newsletters must be written and the emails sent regardless of the time or day. That's not a complaint. It's just part of the job—a double job—that covers the mission field and our supporters back home.

Home. Where is my home now? I've been on the mission field for almost four decades and I wonder if I could adapt to living in the States again. I'm grateful to be able to return periodically to visit my family and the churches and people who support me. The United States moves at a much faster pace than Thailand and Burma. There is always something new and interesting to see. I thoroughly enjoy my trips back, but I wonder if I could live there permanently.

As time goes on, many things change. People change, too. One trip back to the States stands out in my mind. A very dear friend had stopped writing. I noticed each time I would visit her at her home to have a meal, our relationship seemed to be changing. It was really disturbing me, so I finally asked her, "What is wrong? What have I done to offend you?" She said, "Nothing! You're a missionary." I asked, "What does that mean?" She said, "Well, you're a missionary." What she was saying was, that because God had called me to the mission field, she had put me up on a pedestal. She thought that she couldn't relate to me anymore. That she wasn't a benefit in my life anymore. That couldn't have been further from the truth. Every letter she wrote to me telling me what the Lord was doing in her life was uplifting and encouraging to me. I remember rejoicing with her through one of her letters as I was reading it while walking down the street in Bangkok. Even though we are far away, we are no different than if we were there. So, we talked about it, cried together, and now our relationship is back to normal. It's not fair for any of us to look at any Christian that's in a leadership position as better or higher than anybody else. We are exactly the same in living with the Lord step by step, whether our mission field is across the world, or in our home with our husband and children. Each one is just as important. I hope that each person who is reading this will understand that, and treat each one God has called to a leadership position as just a regular person, a regular servant for the Lord, just as they are. Your continuing friendship and love mean more than you will ever know.

As I've hopefully made clear throughout this book, learning new languages has pretty much been the biggest challenge of my missionary existence. I would have loved it if the Lord had called me to a mission field with a language that uses ABC letters. I have often wondered why He would call me to a situation like this, but I guess it's another of His ways of showing us that when we are weak, He is strong. It proves that none of it comes from me, and it all comes from Him.

The first language that I had to learn was Karen, since those were the people I was called to serve and disciple. I couldn't speak one word, other than "Jesus loves you," for three years.

That was a tremendous struggle and source of frustration for me, but I knew that God had called me to those people, and if the language was a problem, He would eventually provide the solution. The solution took years, but I am so thankful for the Lord enabling me to learn. As I write this the Lord is having me learn another language, Thai. I wouldn't have thought it possible, but Thai is actually harder for me to learn than Karen. It has more tones than the high, low, short, and long tones in the Karen language. Thai words have tones that go up and down, down and up, short and long, high and low, and it's all over the place. I wasn't expecting this kind of major challenge at this stage of my life, but by now maybe I should have learned to expect the unexpected from the Lord. Sometimes I have dreams of being able to go back and minister in English, and I'd feel so free. And yet, if that's not what the Lord has called me to do, I know that I would be miserable if I did something because it was easy, not because it was what I was called to do. I will continue to persevere, and praise him for each new word I learn. (And sometimes it really does feel like I'm learning them one at a time.) With each new word I move forward to be better able to minister to the Karen, Thai, and all the people in this part of the world.

Obviously, learning languages has been one of my longest trials, but it is intellectual, not physical. In the numerous attacks on my body, my first bout with malaria was certainly one of the hardest. I was taking malaria prevention medicine at the time, so I had no thoughts of getting it. The head of the village school, Lionel, suggested I travel from Bangkok to visit the Karen in the north, so off I went. We had a wonderful time traveling and evangelizing in many villages. By the time I returned to Bangkok, the roads were open to Htee Hta, so Lionel arranged for a truck to take me in the next day. That afternoon I fainted for the first, and only, time in my life. The guesthouse where I was staying took good care of me, so I was better the next day. However, on my way back to the village, I weakened. By the time I arrived to the first village, I didn't feel well at all. I arrived to Htee Hta village the next day, where they checked my blood and found out I had malaria. By then I was too sick to be taken out again. They started the malaria treatment, but the bug already had a firm grip on me. I got really sick, and to make a bad situation worse, the malaria medication caused me to hallucinate and I couldn't eat anything. I told them I wanted to stop taking the medication and they said okay, but that I could die. That's really not a very good choice. This was their concern from the beginning, so I didn't dare stop taking the medication. On the positive side, it was at this difficult point that I met Daniel Zu, who became and remains my closest spiritual partner. God brings people into our lives on His timetable, not ours, and His timing is always right.

On the seventh day, after my last pill, they arranged for a truck to take me back to Bangkok. Lionel's wife, Esther, was there recuperating from malaria herself. She did her best to make sure I was fed well, but all I could think of was getting to the United States. I called my children, my mom, and my friend, Ron Case. I told them all I was going back and told my mom to have a hospital bed ready for me with clean sheets in an air-conditioned room. This surely shows how spoiled I was and I clearly had an attitude problem. I was disappointed with the Lord, because I thought He would never allow me to get malaria. He knows what a baby I am when it comes to pain, so why would He allow me to get that horrible disease? I knew I never wanted to get it again, so I decided I would return to the safety of the States.

That night I told the Lord, if it was not His will for me to go back to America, then He needed to show me *clearly* in His Word—black and white with no loopholes. I knew I would take any loophole I could find. The next morning, I had my regular quiet time. I continued my Bible reading where I had left off the preceding day, which "just happened" to be Luke 14. The passage, Luke 14:27 and 33 says, "If anyone comes to Me and does not hate [love Jesus more than] his father and mother, wife and children, brothers and sisters, yes, and his own life also, he cannot be My disciple. Whoever of you does not forsake all that he has cannot be My disciple." Hate my own life . . . forsake all that I have . . . that would mean giving up comfort and health . . . black and white with no loopholes. So, now what? Calls to America again. Never mind, the Lord wants me to stay here. I'm staying here.

I told the Lord, "Okay, but You need to change my heart. I want to obey You, but I don't want to go back to the village." It took six weeks to recuperate from the malaria. After I was strong again, they arranged a truck to take me back to Htee Hta village. I didn't think much about it until we passed through the village gate, then I realized I was so excited to be back. I understood the Lord had answered my prayer of Psalm 51:10-12, "Create in me a clean heart, O God, and renew a steadfast spirit within me. Do not cast me away from Your presence, and do not take Your Holy Spirit from me. Restore to me the joy of Your salvation, and uphold me by Your generous Spirit." I had lost the joy of my salvation and it worried me, but the Lord restored it a hundredfold. What a wonderful blessing and miracle of the Lord to have His joy and a clean heart again. Words cannot express it.

Those of us who work in the spiritual realm understand that

there are malevolent spiritual beings—demons—as well as good ones. The book of Genesis tells us that one third of the angels rebelled with Satan and continue to attack us. Those of us who work in the spiritual realm don't have to go looking for demons. Sometimes they come to us. Such was the case at the women's prison.

After I taught the women inmates the Bible, many wanted to be baptized. I asked Pastor Moses to come teach them about baptism. Many decided to be baptized, and the prison agreed to allow them to go to a nearby river for the ceremony. Everyone was looking forward to the big event. Well, if you want to rile up dark spiritual forces, a surefire way of doing it is to bring someone closer to the Lord. As the date for the baptismal service approached, one woman began to suffer bouts of severe physical shaking. There could certainly be medical reasons for this, of course, but previous experience had led us to believe it was more likely they were spiritual attacks. We proceeded to fervently pray against these "fits," and sure enough, they lessened until she only had attacks on Sunday during the Bible study. That confirmed our belief. Finally, the day of their baptism arrived and she was fine in the morning, but when it was time to go to the river, she had another fit. I asked the prison guards if they would carry her down to the river, but they said to leave her alone. At this point I had another attitude problem. I was grumbling in my heart (while praying, of course) because I wanted her to be baptized with the others. The Lord quickly convicted me and urged me to go and rejoice with those who were being baptized. I obeyed Him and continued to pray as I walked toward the river, my heart truly rejoicing. Suddenly, I looked up and saw her coming on her own—no more fits—and smiling. What a praise to know the Lord healed her just in time.

People who go looking for dark spiritual forces will

frequently find them. In areas where the occult is practiced, or false gods are worshiped, it's not unusual to see some strange, often frightening, things. One thing is certain, where there is a great deal of spiritual darkness you can expect it to attack the light. We had a chilling case of this at the village school. For no apparent reason, the girls living in the dorm suddenly started acting very strangely. They were crying, laughing, angry, hitting, and hysterical all at the same time—completely out of control. Someone said that a curse had been put on them. I don't know who, or how, but I'd never seen anything like it before. It was truly a disturbing manifestation. The church leaders immediately prayed for them, but the bizarre, uncontrolled emotional outbursts continued. The girls were not one bit better. That's when I was asked to pray for them.

In the Roman Catholic Church, when an extreme demonic manifestation appears, especially trained priests conduct an exorcism. I am by no means an exorcist, but I chose to trust the Lord. He has power over all spirits and evil. I also understand from Matthew 17:20-21 that some of these manifestations are more difficult to deal with than others. The Lord gave me the verses in James 5:14-16, "Is anyone among you sick? Let him call for the elders of the church, and let them pray over him, anointing him with oil in the name of the Lord. And the prayer of faith will save the sick, and the Lord will raise him up. And if he has committed sins, he will be forgiven. Confess your sins to one another, and pray for one another." With those verses to guide me, I spent much time seeking the Lord beforehand and asked for the strongest Christian in the village to go to the dorm with me. I enlisted the support of the children in my house, asking them to pray for us until we returned. None of us realized that would be four hours later.

First, I prayed all around the dorm, then went inside and

read James 5:14-16 to everyone. Through my interpreter, I asked them to confess any sins, then anointed them with oil and prayed for them. We did this one by one. All of the girls were giggling and nervous before their turn, and I was getting annoyed at their distraction. Then the Lord showed me that those who had already been prayed for had settled down and were quiet. I realized the distraction was from the enemy and kept praying for them one by one. After all had confessed their sins and were prayed for, they were healed! A few of the girls were in the village hospital and still causing disturbances, so we went to minister to them the same way and they were healed. John 4:4, ". . . because He who is in you is greater than he who is in the world."

Not all of my trials were of the dark, foreboding type. Some were just, well, very different from what I was used to. As God equipped me for the mission field, one of the most important tools He gave me was a sense of humor. If we can laugh at our circumstances, and especially at ourselves, the stress of our lives is diminished. My former comfortable life in suburban Southern California was absolutely no preparation for the challenges I would find with the Karen in Burma and Thailand. Many of them involved adapting to the culture of the people. Others involved adapting to the jungle and the culture of its animal inhabitants. You can't reason with animals. You'd better have a sense of humor.

My home in Southern California was typical of the American standard of living. Doors, windows and screens, heat and air-conditioning, and running water were all taken for granted, and I had a measure of privacy. In my new home, the realm of humans tended to blend in with our animal neighbors, frequently in startling and inconvenient ways, and frequently at night. I got an early introduction to middle of the night visits from the local animal community. I had not been living in Htee Hta village for very long, so new experiences were abundant. The accommodations in my new home were typically basic; we slept on wooden beds with a straw mat on top. An important part of my "bedroom suite" was a mosquito net. Aside from the buzzing-stinging-itching interruption of a night's sleep, mosquitoes also spread malaria. In that sense, mosquitoes were not just pests, but potentially dangerous pests. With my mosquito net securely fastened around my bed I would be protected from anything getting at me. At least, that was the theory.

Many of our students come from other villages, so they need a place to stay while attending classes. We put everyone up as best we could, and there was no real expectation of privacy. On one particular night there were two new students sharing my room with me. I was sleeping on my wooden bed and they were camping out on the floor. That sounds primitive by American standards, but it was not unusual in that culture. They were happy to go to school, I was happy to teach them, and we were all happy to have a roof over our heads. I was sleeping peacefully until I heard a strange noise. The jungle is full of noises, but this was one I couldn't identify. Our brains are marvelous creations of God that work all the time to determine what we can ignore and what we can't. I guess that's how people in large cities can sleep through the all-night sounds of traffic. Anyway, the sound I heard was not normal and that got my attention. I wasn't alarmed or frightened, just curious. In fact, I was just curious enough to keep from getting any sleep while I tried to figure out what that strange noise was. In my mind I tried to envision what it could be. I lay there for a long time listening before I decided it sounded like a cat chewing on a suitcase strap. Why I came to that conclusion I don't know, but that's what I thought. I couldn't go back to sleep, I just kept listening to the noise. I didn't want to go rustling around and wake the girls up, but finally I'd had enough and decided to investigate. We always keep a flashlight next to us at night because of things like this, and because a trip to the bathroom involved going outside. I rolled over, grabbed it, and shined the beam around the room. I couldn't believe what I saw. On top of my pillow, *inside* my supposedly protective mosquito net next to my head, was a huge cat looking down at me as he chewed on a dead rat! That's not the kind of surprise anyone needs in the middle of the night. And no wonder I couldn't go back to sleep—it was right in my ear. That needed to be dealt with immediately, so I shooed the cat away and he fled under the bed with the rat still in his mouth.

Okay, now what? Underneath the bed were many boxes and suitcases, and he stuck himself right in the middle, and continued to chew on the rat. I thought, *Well, at least they're out of the mosquito net, surely I can go back to sleep now.* Wrong. Because of the constant chewing noise right under my bed, I couldn't sleep, so I finally got up, crawled around on the floor, and shooed the cat out again. He left the rat behind. I went back to bed and as I was finally drifting off to sleep, the cat came back and started chewing on the rat again. I thought, *What can I do? Am I going to let this keep me up all night?* By this point, any affection I may have had for cats was quickly dwindling. I got up again, found some paper, used it to pick up the rat, and threw it out of a small window in the bamboo wall. Then I picked up the intruding cat, and gave him the same treatment. From that time on it never came back. I will never forget the image of looking up and seeing that huge cat and rat right next to my head inside the mosquito net, and actually picking up that rat. And all the time the struggle with the cat went on, the two girls slept soundly on the floor next to the bed. That's one my favorite stories; it adds another dimension to tales of missionary life.

It's really amazing to me the number of creatures God put in our world, some big, some small. And, for some reason, He decided not to put the same creatures everywhere. That's part of the adventure of travel. When we see different parts of the world, we also see different kinds of animals. We don't always think too much about the ones we are accustomed to seeing, but being exposed to new ones can be fascinating, or frightening, or both. I've had friends come to visit who have been afraid of things like frogs when they encountered them in my bathroom. You don't expect frogs in your bathroom in Southern California, but here it's not unusual. Frogs are tiny to me, so I'm not afraid of them, but as they say, sometimes size matters. One day I was walking through the village to visit friends. They weren't in their house, so I started walking down the hill on a very narrow path to the riverbank to see if they were there washing their clothes, or bathing. As I was walking to the river, I suddenly realized that I was being followed. I turned to discover that my friend's cows had decided to accompany me on my walk. I didn't have anything against cows, but I also didn't have much experience with them. Cows are big. I speeded up a little bit, and so did they, which I found a bit alarming. I could picture them walking faster and faster until they trampled me. I thought, *This is the end of my story . . . missionary killed by cows walking down to the river.* I turned around and tried to figure how to go back, or how to get around the cows, but I couldn't see a way that didn't involve pushing them out of my path. Given their size and the number of them, I was pretty sure that wasn't going to work. The only thing I could do was keep going with the cows right on my heels. Eventually I came to the river and I was trapped; nowhere to run, and my friends weren't there to help me. But God put His angels around me, and protected me. I turned to face the cows, but they walked past me and began drinking at the river. I slowly edged my way back up the hill and scrambled back to safety.

The malaria-spreading mosquitoes aren't the only small creatures that can be problematic, and sometimes the small ones are hard to avoid. I had just finished bathing in the private bathroom at my home in Ah Moe village one day, dressed in a sarong, since we are never fully exposed. I got my towel down off the hook and dried what I could of my body, arms, and face, when I felt a stabbing pain—a sting. I looked at my towel, which was the perfect shade of brown to conceal the scorpion that was lurking on it. I immediately dropped the towel, but it was too late. He had gotten me. A scorpion sting is excruciatingly painful, so I knew what I was in for. With my lip in agony, I quickly changed into my dry sarong, and burst out the door. Many people came to help me, but nothing they put on my lip eased the pain. I asked if they had any aloe vera and they brought some from the mission school up the hill. I quickly applied it. They advised me to lie down, be calm, and rest. I guess that made sense to them, but as long as I did that, I had nothing to focus on but the pain. I told them that I needed to get up and go do something—think about something else—so I went up to the school and started talking to the students. I was quite a sight with my lip totally swollen. Everyone asked about it, but I forced myself to concentrate on them and not on the pain. That little creature caused me a great deal of misery, but in God's timing, the pain went away.

It could've been worse. I've only been bitten by scorpions

twice, which I think is amazing, considering that the little devils are everywhere. Compare that with my oldest daughter, Kelly, and her husband, Dave, who seemed to be scorpion magnets. They attracted scorpions everywhere they turned. They picked up a book, and scorpions were there; they'd grab a towel, and scorpions were there. Scorpions came out of the walls in their room. One time Dave was teaching and a mother scorpion and her babies fell on the book he was teaching from in front of the classroom. I'm glad scorpions have not been attracted to me, as they were to them. Given the choice between the two, I suppose I would have to pick cows.

When you're in an unfamiliar culture, something as simple as a meal can become an adventure. I was visiting the Ah Moe Mission School dining room one time when Daniel Zu and some other teachers were eating lunch. I had already eaten, but I was nibbling at some of the dishes set out on the table. I had reached the point where I needed to wear glasses for reading, but not for walking around. I wasn't reading at the table so I didn't have my glasses on, and I thought a bowl of green things next to me were green beans. We eat with our hands in the village, so I just picked up a bunch of them and popped them in my mouth. As I did this, I noticed a look of shock on Daniel Zu's face. He opened his mouth to cry out, but it was too late; I put them in too quickly. I was about to ask him what was wrong, but as I began to chew, I knew immediately. I had just bitten into an entire handful of fresh, green chili peppers. A chili pepper or two can be pretty uncomfortable, but an entire handful of them was beyond belief. I felt like my mouth was a furnace. My eyes and nose were watering and I was struggling to catch my breath. Daniel had students running all over the place bringing packages of milk, sugar, salt, water, and anything else he could think of that might ease the pain. Nothing worked very well, so I had to just endure it. Lesson learned. From that day on I always wore my glasses. I didn't care if I didn't need them for walking around or not, I started wearing them all the time. There are certain things that you really, really don't want to do more than once. My daughter Shelly and my coworker Shaune have done the same thing, so I feel less foolish about it.

The Lord likes His servants to be humble, and if we forget, He will arrange to remind us. That was the case when Daniel Zu decided that he wanted to meet our main mission school funder who had supported the school building project. Daniel was concerned because he had no legal papers to allow him to travel in Thailand, but I challenged him to trust the Lord. That is not something I will ever do again. When I take a risk it's one thing, but encouraging someone else to do so is something else. Daniel ended up being arrested and put in jail. I insisted the police take me with him, which they did, but they ignored my pleas to release him. I called everyone I knew for help. I even called our mission school funder, but all of the high authorities he knew couldn't help, because President Clinton was visiting the country and everyone was focused on his security.

I finally left the jail after they promised me Daniel would still be there in the morning. I couldn't sleep. Another friend with us, a Thai college professor, couldn't sleep, either. We went back to the jail to take Daniel some food and my Bible. I will never forget the scene when we arrived at midnight. There he was, with all of the other prisoners sitting around him in a circle, sharing the Gospel with them, just like I picture the apostle Paul did. The policeman decided to show his authority and told us he wouldn't give him anything we brought, but I peeked back around the corner as we were leaving and I saw him giving Daniel my Bible. God's amazing grace.

The next morning, when we returned to the police station, he was gone! They had moved him to the huge immigration jail. The Thai professor was able to stand in line and see him without any trouble, but I had only a photocopy of my passport, which they wouldn't accept, so I had to go to the mission's office and bring back the original. This took over an hour, so I had no idea where Daniel or the Thai professor were. I just followed the crowd as they let us in and Daniel saw me. Amazingly, he asked me if I could get ten of them out. So many were asking him about my Bible because it has a cross stiched on the front of it. He had been sharing the Gospel and wanted to help them, but I didn't know how we were going to get Daniel out, let alone another nine people. I told him I needed to find the Thai professor, hoping I would be able to get back and see Daniel again. The professor ended up finding me, rather than the other way around, and the Thai were asking her if she could help in sending Daniel and nine others to the jail in Kanchanaburi, which is the closest town to where we lived. I couldn't believe it. It would cost a little money, but I had enough and said we would gladly cooperate. This was so miraculous that I knew the Lord was with us. She gave the money to the Thai authorities, found out what time they would be leaving, and went to get the others with us to follow the police van. They told me to go back to the village and wait for them there. I knew this was wise, so I took public transportation back, prayed and waited, and prayed and waited some more. I began to really worry as it began to get dark and prayed even more fervently. They showed up a few minutes later—what a wonderful, miraculous reunion. The story of how they rescued Daniel would make an excellent, suspenseful movie. Only the Lord could have organized and accomplished this.

Daniel's one prayer was to be reunited with his family and home in time for their wedding anniversary the next day. With him freed from jail, and back to the Thai border, we set out on foot. We scurried up the mountain as I prayed for the Lord to hold the descending darkness back. I can see nothing in the dark, no one had flashlights, and the terrain was treacherous. The Lord held the time back, reminding me of the Lord's miracle in Isaiah 38:7. "And this is the sign to you from the Lord . . . which He has spoken, 'I will bring the shadow of the sundial, which is gone down with the sun on the sundial of Ahaz degrees backwards.' So the sun returned on the dial ten degrees." I knew this story in the Bible and prayed for the Lord to do this miracle for us, and He did. He is so faithful. Daniel was home right at midnight, God's perfect timing for his wedding anniversary, and thanking the Lord for answering his prayers.

My life has been an adventure. There have been good things, and bad things that were learning experiences. And there were also a few things, like my bad advice to Daniel and that bowl of chili peppers, that have kept me humble.

CHAPTER TWELVE

FORWARD WITH FAITH AND GRATITUDE

O Lord, You are my God. I will exalt You, I will praise Your name,
for You have done wonderful things;
Your counsels of old are faithfulness and truth.

Isaiah 25:1

Why would God send one woman into a jungle war zone by herself to minister for Him? I still cannot answer that question, other than I know that He did it. Maybe it was because He knew I *could/would* go. The only thing I can think of in scripture that might relate to this is in Acts 10, when the Holy Spirit directs Peter to go to the house of Cornelius, a Gentile and a centurion, and minister to him. For a Jew to go into the house of a Gentile was strictly forbidden. Cornelius's house was to Peter as the jungle was to me. It was not a place he would ever choose to go, but he went because God told him to. Or when God's angel told Phillip to go to the eunuch in Gaza. Only God knows where the needs are, who He wants to go to them, and when His perfect timing is. (Acts 8:26-39)

I believe that every Christian has their own, special assignment from God. For some, it's standing before hundreds or thousands of people and proclaiming the Word of God. For others, it may be showing kindness and compassion to the poor, sick, homeless, and oppressed. It could be raising your children to be loving Christians, who show that love of God through their actions their entire lives. Whatever assignment God gives us is ours alone, and He doesn't compare or judge our accomplishments to those of others. The person whose assignment it is to care for a few homeless receives the same acknowledgment from God as the person whose assignment is to preach before thousands. Our relationship with God is individual, just as our lives are.

By 1985 I thought I had found my assignment. I was enjoying wonderful Christian fellowship in my church with my daughters, and housing ministry at my church, taking in women in need. If that was all that God had for me to do, I would have been perfectly happy. However, God's vision was far greater than mine. From the moment He spoke to my heart during that church slide presentation, He was directing my life. It took me a little while to realize that, but once I understood, I gladly—if sometimes apprehensively—went wherever He led me. The road was not always smooth, but He carried me over the rough spots.

Over the decades, I have had so many experiences, both good and bad. In some cases, they would have been terrifying had I not had the firm knowledge that God had sent me on this mission, therefore, He would protect me. I focus on the good memories. The evangelism trips down the river when we were in Kaw Thoo Lei were probably the highlights for all of us. They were adventurous and challenging. The dirt road was full of bumps, holes, and mud. In the rainy season there would be big logging trucks stuck in the mud under the weight of their loads, completely blocking traffic. We couldn't get past them, so the river became our road. We used it to get in and out of the villages. We used it to get almost everywhere. Every single journey was an adventure. We went up and downriver many times for evangelism, getting supplies, taking patients to the hospital in another village, and many other reasons. When the water was low in the dry season, it was very rocky. The boats would tip over if the driver didn't know how to negotiate around the rocks. Imagine if your trip to the grocery store might involve getting dumped into a river. I remember praying one time, asking the Lord to take my eyes off the circumstances, and put them on Him. I was afraid only one time when we were going by boat. The rapids were strong and there was much debris in the river. He was able to keep me focused on Him which relieved my anxiety. Normally I was not concerned, even in the rainy season when the river was faster than normal. Most of the other people were afraid, but we didn't have to worry about the rocks, and we got there fast. On those trips, it was actually fun for me.

I remember in the beginning, writing my adventures in my newsletters, and having people comment, "You know, we can't even relate. You don't even need to go into all that detail in your newsletters." I was sent to a part of the world that was beyond the imagination of my stateside friends. It was just the most amazing thing, and I have been grateful for almost all of it. (I could have foregone malaria, car accidents, scorpions, and miscellaneous jungle diseases, but you know what I mean.) What a difference from my former privileged, Southern California life.

My time among the Karen in Burma and Thailand was a constant learning experience that continues to this day. When we went to other villages, even Daniel Zu had to be cognizant of cultural differences. Each village can be different with different customs even though it's the same tribe of people. I could never just learn the Karen culture and go on my way. The Karen culture was actually many cultures, slightly different from one another, and enormously different from the culture in which I was raised. The language was mostly the same, but food, bathing, and a multitude of small things might be different. I had to stay on my toes to make sure I didn't inadvertently offend someone. Who eats first? How do they eat? What can you say and what can't you say? That was probably one of my biggest challenges after I learned the language. It was difficult enough speaking that unfamiliar language without having the fear that I would say something wrong or be misunderstood.

I was so grateful to Daniel Zu for helping me when he first arrived there, from the very beginning until we fled from the Burmese Army together. Daniel has become a blessing for so many. He had a hard time being head of the mission school; it was really a trial for him. Later we knew it was God's training ground for him to prepare for the next ministry God gave him as leader of 10,000 refugees inside Tham Hin refugee camp. When you show God you are faithful in small things, He will give you greater things. I think throughout our lives we're definitely in training for something that only God knows is up ahead. I love being on an adventure with God.

The Karen children, that the Lord gave me so many years ago, are now all grown up. My last single daughter was married in May 2003 and my sons are all married now. It's exciting to see them grow up and become adults serving and loving the Lord. It's hard to be a discipler. I could have been an evangelist and gone from village to village, then returned home. Then my human faults would not be exposed. As a discipler they see me twenty-four hours a day. My human characteristics, good and bad, are revealed to all. This is God's plan, I suppose, to show I am a human being saved by God's mercy, just like them. The grace of God and the Karen are amazing. No matter what they've seen me go through, and no matter what I've seen them go through, we continue to love each other. I'm really blessed that God has given us each other.

My life has been an endless collection of big and small miracles. I didn't always recognize them when they were happening, but looking back, I can clearly see them now. In America I raised my children wondering where the money would come from, and was then bewildered (and grateful) when my expenses were met, even though they exceeded my income. I went to a jungle village where I didn't know the language, the customs, the food, or how to get along without transportation, newspapers, or phones. Nevertheless, I survived and discipled the Karen children the Lord gave me. I have never regretted giving my life to the Lord. I don't know why I waited for thirty years. I'd gone to Sunday school from the time I was five years old, and I knew right from wrong. Life would have been a lot easier had I given in sooner. But again, God has His perfect timing. I've learned not to question Him.

On my occasional trips back to the United States, I speak at churches and meet many wonderful people. They hear my story of how a short, spunky young woman left her sheltered life, travelled to the other side of the world alone, and served a jungle tribe for decades until she became a shorter—and still spunky—senior citizen. "Why did you go there?" they sometimes ask. I can give them long answers, short answers, extensive details, or no details, but the answer really only requires three words: God sent me.

But none of these things move me; nor do I count my life dear to myself,
so that I may finish my race with joy, and the ministry
which I received from the Lord Jesus,
to testify to the gospel of the grace of God.

Acts 20:24

EPILOGUE

Tragically, the atrocities of the Burmese military are ongoing to this day. As this book is completed in 2022, a new assault against the Karen is in progress, but the attackers are no longer just soldiers with rifles. The situation is worse because the Burmese military has airplanes and helicopters, and is bombing all nationalities that oppose the new government that seized power in a coup in 2021. They mercilessly gather people and burn them alive. Thousands are in hiding in caves and makeshift shelters made from anything they can find in the jungle. They have to protect themselves not just from their tormentors, but from monsoon rains, unrelenting heat, and brutal humidity. Thousands have also managed to flee into Thailand again, which makes it difficult, since the military Thai leaders work with the Burmese military. Please pray for their safety, for the ongoing atrocities to stop, and for God's time to arise soon!

"Behold, the LORD's hand is not shortened,
That it cannot save;
Nor His ear heavy,
That it cannot hear."

Isaiah 59:1

"For the oppression of the poor, for the sighing of the needy,
Now I will arise," says the LORD;
"I will set him in the safety for which he yearns."

Psalm 12:5

The work continues

ABOUT THE AUTHORS

Sharon Porterfield

Born in Southern California to atheist parents, as a young adult, Sharon Porterfield became a Christian at the age of thirty. In her mid-forties she knew she had been called to serve, and has spent her life in the jungles of Southeast Asia as a missionary to the Karen people.

To live is Christ.
Philippians 1:21

Douglas Wellman

Douglas Wellman was a television producer-director in Hollywood for over thirty years, and Assistant Dean of the School of Cinematic Arts at the University of Southern California. Now retired, he is a Christian minister and works as a chaplain at a Southern Utah hospital. He is the co-author of *Boxes: The Secret Life of Howard Hughes, Five Minutes, Mr. Byner!* and *Surviving Hiroshima: A Young Woman's Story* (and the upcoming *A Teenaged Girl in Auschwitz.*)

OTHER BOOKS
CO-AUTHORED BY
DOUGLAS WELLMAN

This second edition of *Boxes: The Secret Life of Howard Hughes* continues the history-changing story of Eva McLelland and her reclusive life married to a mystery man she discovered was Howard Hughes. New witnesses have come forward with personal stories, additional evidence, and photographs. Hughes's links to the murder of mobster Bugsy Siegel and the killers of President John F. Kennedy are revealed as well as the real identity of the long-haired crazy man that Hughes placed in the Desert Inn Hotel to distract the world while he escaped. Eva McLelland kept her secret for thirty-one stressful years as she lived a nomadic existence with a man who refused to unpack his belongings for fear he would be discovered and have to flee. Only her husband's death finally released her to tell the story that had been burning inside her for decades.

John Byner is a man of many voices and characters, from impersonating the slow, rolling gait and speech of John Wayne, to lending his voice to The Ant and the Aardvark cartoons. His dead-on impersonations, as well as his unique talents as a character actor, have put him on the small screen in peoples' homes, the big screen in theaters, and no screen on Broadway.

Growing up in a big family on Long Island, John discovered his uncanny ability to mimic voices as a child when he returned home from a Bing Crosby movie and repeated Bing's performance for his family in their living room. He discovered his talent made him the focus of everyone's attention, and allowed him to make friends wherever he went, from elementary school to the U.S. Navy.

John started his career in nightclubs in New York, but soon found himself getting national acclaim on The Ed Sullivan Show. With that he was on his way. This memoir is the best and funniest moments of his life, career, and relationships with some of the biggest names in entertainment, both on and off the screen.

On August 6, 1945, 22-year-old Kaleria Pachikoff was doing pre-breakfast chores when a blinding flash lit the sky over Hiroshima, Japan. A moment later, everything went black as the house collapsed on her and her family. Their world, and everyone else's, changed as the first atomic bomb was detonated over a city.

From Russian nobility, the Palchikoff's barely escaped death at the hands of Bolshevik revolutionaries until her father, a White Russian officer, hijacked a ship to take them to safety in Hiroshima. Safety was short lived. Her father, a talented musician, established a new life for the family, but the outbreak of World War II created a cloud of suspicion that led to his imprisonment and years of deprivation for his family.

After the bombing, trapped in the center of previously unimagined devastation, Kaleria summoned her strength to come to the aid of bomb victims, treating the never-before seen effects of radiation.

Fluent in English, Kaleria was soon recruited to work with Gen. Douglas MacArthur's occupation forces in a number of secretarial positions until the family found a new life in the United States.

Heavily based on quotes from Kaleria's memoirs written immediately after World War II, and transcripts of United States Army Air Force interviews with her, her story is an emotional, and sometime chilling, story of courage and survival in the face of one of history's greatest catastrophes.